Praise for *The Idea Is the Easy Part*

"Venture capital is a uniquely American institution, and Brian Dovey is a practitioner of the highest rank. Anyone interested in starting a business or investing in venture capital should read this book. What you will learn here is invaluable. Brian will help you understand the numbers and will inspire you to listen for the music—to recognize what has never been done before can happen with a particular founder. Ultimately venture capital is a very human enterprise and Brian has honed his humanity as well as his technical understanding. That is why he is such a big success. And now he shares it all with his readers. And success couldn't happen to a nicer person."

> —Bill Bradley, former U.S. Senator and investment banker

"In *The Idea is the Easy Part*, veteran venture capitalist Brian Dovey confronts myths about entrepreneurs, startups, and *Shark Tank* as he challenges would-be business owners to look before they leap. Encouraging and thought provoking, this book is a great read."

> —Ken Blanchard, coauthor of *Simple Truths of Leadership* and *Leading at a Higher Level*

"*The Idea is the Easy Part* is an honest and realistic look at the challenges and rewards of entrepreneurship. I highly recommend this book to anyone considering starting a business."

> —Chris Barton, Founder of Shazam, three-time entrepreneur, inventor, and tech investor

"It is so well done. The topics are spot on, the content and examples so pertinent. It's easy to read but the rich, deep insight is incredible. I want to pre-order many copies for gifts."

> —Bonnie Anderson, Executive Chairman, Veracyte

"They say that common sense is very uncommon, but analyzing a problem and defining it correctly is necessary before common sense can be applied. In my mind, that is what makes this project unique. The book is well written and understandable—no jargon, technical terms, or words one has to look up. It's an easy read, which is essential. Well done!"

> —Richard Schiding, former President, Vasont Systems

"Brian's storytelling approach is so helpful because it is real-world experience filled with context and color. He brings readers into the stories so that we can appreciate the information we would experience under the same circumstances. Further, the myth-busting is entertaining. I laughed more than a few times."

—Mary Fisher, CEO, Colorescience

"If you want another rah-rah book that reinforces old myths or a detailed how-to book, look elsewhere. But if you want an excellent, realistic, straight-talking, often amusing introduction to the entrepreneurial world, you've come to the right place."

—Brook Byers, Cofounder, Kleiner Perkins Caufield & Byers

"Brian Dovey is a master storyteller. He dispenses profound wisdom about the entrepreneurship process based on his involvement in more than 300 new ventures as an investor, board member. and entrepreneur. He generously shares his thought processes on a wide range of issues that come up in any type of startup venture. He truly is an educator at heart."

—Alex DeNoble, Professor of Management,
San Diego State University

"This should be well received because it doesn't repeat the prevailing wisdom. It avoids the trap of providing dozens of war stories to make your points and avoids generalities."

—Jim Blair, Domain Associates

THE
IDEA
IS THE
EASY
PART

THE IDEA IS THE EASY PART

Myths and Realities of the Startup World

BRIAN DOVEY

Matt Holt Books
An Imprint of BenBella Books, Inc.
Dallas, TX

Matt Holt is an imprint of BenBella Books, Inc.
10440 N. Central Expressway
Suite 800
Dallas, TX 75231
benbellabooks.com
Send feedback to feedback@benbellabooks.com

BenBella and *Matt Holt* are federally registered trademarks.

Printed in the United States of America
10 9 8 7 6 5 4 3 2 1

Library of Congress Control Number: 2023005839
ISBN 9781637744048 (hardcover)
ISBN 9781637744055 (electronic)

Copyediting by Lydia Choi
Proofreading by Denise Pangia and Lisa Story
Indexing by WordCo Indexing Services, Inc.
Text design and composition by PerfecType, Nashville, TN
Cover design by Brigid Pearson
Printed by Lake Book Manufacturing

To my wonderful family, who encouraged, cajoled, and otherwise supported me.

CONTENTS

CONTENTS

FOREWORD

Brook Byers, cofounder, Kleiner Perkins Caufield & Byers

Back in the early 1970s, most venture capitalists were experts in finance who focused on carefully analyzing a startup's business model. The conventional wisdom was that if you could accurately predict future growth and profitability, it would become clear whether that startup was worthy of a VC investment, and at what valuation.

But Gene Kleiner and Tom Perkins saw things from a different perspective. They came from significant operational leadership roles at tech companies, not from Wall Street. They were experienced at rolling up their sleeves and solving startup problems rather than scrutinizing balance sheets and P&L projections. So, when they launched their own VC firm, they put a premium on execution and operational excellence. They knew, as Brian Dovey puts it in this insightful book, that *the idea is the easy part*.

Gene and Tom taught Frank Caufield and me that methodology. Whenever we evaluated a startup, we looked beyond its big idea and potential market to whether the founders had the necessary skills to maximize the potential of their idea. As we grew our

VC firm over the next few decades, we added more partners with significant operating experience. And we helped entrepreneurs build more than one thousand companies that created countless new products and at least two million jobs.

In any decade and any economic conditions, launching and sustaining a startup is incredibly hard. While the planning process is a key step toward success, and business plans are essential, they can only take you so far. As Mike Tyson memorably put it, "Everyone has a plan till they get punched in the mouth." The world's best plan won't save you unless you also get good at problem-solving, execution, management, operations, and pivoting when necessary. We distinguished KPCB by offering founders our best advice in those areas and working shoulder to shoulder to assist them rather than merely opening our checkbook.

Brian, whom I've been delighted to know for more than three decades, epitomizes this execution-driven approach to launching and growing startups. He offers a unique blend of insights, rules of thumb, and true stories that I haven't seen in other books. He breaks down the most common myths about entrepreneurship and shows what it really takes to make a startup viable in an ambiguous environment with barely adequate resources.

Brian has accumulated an enviable range of experiences, from startups and Fortune 500 companies to a thriving VC firm, Domain Associates. He's the first to admit that a lot of his experiences have included mistakes, and some of his initiatives were outright failures. But he also knows that mistakes and failures make the best teachers. His diverse experiences make this book very different from most sources of startup advice, which tend to focus on famous success stories.

People love to hear about young, idealistic founders who changed the world while enjoying global fame and unimaginable wealth. Which is understandable—I love those stories, too. But if you're thinking about starting a company in 2023 and beyond, you're much better off with a more realistic guide, drawing on examples you've probably never heard of, including some that went belly-up.

I wish all startup founders, and aspiring ones, would read *The Idea Is the Easy Part*. If they do, they will probably develop a more grounded set of ambitions and a clearer sense of what they need to do to achieve those ambitions. In my experience, big ideas and capital are easier to find than entrepreneurs who know how to make the most of those resources. This book can help you become one of those exceptionally valuable entrepreneurs.

If you want another rah-rah book that reinforces old myths, or a detailed how-to book, look elsewhere. But if you want an excellent, realistic, straight-talking, often amusing introduction to the entrepreneurial world, you've come to the right place.

Brook Byers
November 2022

INTRODUCTION

This book spent many years kicking around inside my head, and on a lot of PowerPoint slides, before I started writing. Its origins go back to the 1990s, when I was still a relatively new venture capitalist, following my earlier careers as a startup founder and then a big-company president. As part of that career pivot, I spent a lot of time thinking about what entrepreneurship is, what it isn't, and why it's so often misunderstood and misrepresented.

I also developed an itch to teach entrepreneurship part-time to the next generation, which I mentioned to my friend Jeff Timmons, dean of the Kauffman Fellows Program (a fantastic non-profit that promotes equal opportunity in the startup world). Jeff introduced me to Alex DeNoble, a professor at San Diego State University, who was gracious enough to let me try co-teaching his entrepreneurship class.

Alex asked what topics I'd like to focus on in the classroom, assuming that a VC would surely pick something like how to choose a startup opportunity, write a business plan, or pitch investors. I surprised him by replying that even though those subjects are important, other aspects of startup life are even more important but get relatively little attention.

At that time (and still to this day), I was hearing a lot of pitches from startup founders who seemed to think that a great idea would automatically bring customers and investors to their door, putting them on a glide path to fame and fortune. They seemed to have no clue that the real challenge was turning an initial idea into an actual, sustainable, profitable company. They couldn't see that *the idea is the easy part!*

So Alex and I developed a new course, "Managing the Growing Firm," which focused on execution, team building, operations, and other practical realities. I illustrated the points I made in lectures with the true stories of successful and not-so-successful startups that my firm had invested in. The class was an immediate hit with students, and Alex and I have been coteaching it ever since.

Meanwhile, however, myths and false impressions about entrepreneurship and startup culture have continued to spread. Fans of "reality TV" shows like *Shark Tank* still think they can make a fortune from a clever idea and a slick elevator pitch. And detractors really think the startup world is full of egomaniacs and dishonest "vulture capitalists." Both camps are very far from reality, as I explain to a new group of SDSU students every semester.

Since spreading an important message one classroom at a time isn't very efficient, I started writing this book. And here it is. I don't pretend to have all the answers, let alone any brilliant, foolproof formula for success. But if this book can help you start your entrepreneurial journey on a foundation of reality instead of mythology, that must be worth something.

The idea is the easy part, but even the hard part—making a company work—is still a lot of fun.

THE ENTREPRENEURIAL MYSTIQUE
Myth Versus Reality

THE MYSTIQUE OF THE STARTUP WORLD

When I was a student at Harvard Business School in the late 1960s, there was only one course on entrepreneurship, called "Management of New Enterprises." The word "entrepreneur" wasn't even in the course title because it carried a negative connotation. Several of my professors said Harvard's mission was to train the future leaders of the Fortune 500, not the heads of trivial little businesses. This perspective was so pervasive that I remained reluctant to call myself an entrepreneur for many years, even after I pivoted from the corporate world to the startup world.

Today, by contrast, Harvard Business School offers at least two dozen courses about startups and requires all MBA students to study entrepreneurship, as do most business schools. Many high schools also offer classes on the subject. Is it any surprise that many of our brightest students want to launch their own businesses someday? Startup founders have become rock stars. Numerous books about the likes of Steve Jobs, Jeff Bezos, and Elon Musk are bestsellers, as are the memoirs of icons like Phil Knight and Richard Branson. As entrepreneurship has evolved from a small niche to the white-hot center of capitalism, an elaborate mystique and mythology has built up around it.

But those books, as well as movies like *The Social Network* and TV shows like *Shark Tank,* make terrible how-to guides to achieving fame and fortune. Most memoirs, movies, and reality shows about founders are heavily fictionalized to attract the widest possible audiences. I'm not saying you shouldn't enjoy them, merely that you can't treat them like a road map. For instance, they often make it seem like it's possible to get immediate funding for a startup with a big idea and a slick, five-minute elevator pitch. And they imply that once you get funding, you're already on the twenty-yard line, on the verge of a touchdown. In reality, getting funding is incredibly hard, and even then you're on *your own* twenty-yard line, with eighty yards still to go. Real success is in making the company self-sustaining.

Although there has never been more content available about startups, much of it is misleading and does a poor job of explaining why they fail or succeed. My goal for this book is to help you, an aspiring (or potentially aspiring) entrepreneur, understand the reality of what you might be getting into and how to navigate this strange world. After decades as a startup leader, big-company executive, and venture capitalist, I've pretty much seen it all. Now I want to share my hard-won insights, advice, and relevant stories with people like you.

The mystique of entrepreneurship isn't entirely positive, of course. Many of the college students I meet hold negative stereotypes about startup life. Some media depictions imply that starting a business requires a complete lack of empathy and a relentless drive to step on, or at least step over, other people to get what you want. In reality, most of the successful entrepreneurs I've worked with are honest and ethical. They just aren't interested in attracting media attention the way a ruthless minority of founders often do.

This book is aiming for the sweet spot between starry-eyed optimism and dour negativity. If you've been seduced by fantasies about an easy path to fame and fortune, I'll try to bring you back down to earth. But if you're skeptical about your qualifications to start and run a company, I'll try to reassure you that you probably already have the skills you need and that you can do a lot of good for the world as an entrepreneur.

THE IDEA IS THE EASY PART

The biggest and most damaging myth of the startup world is that a successful startup requires an innovative new product or service: *it's all about the big idea!* Every business experience I've ever had points to the opposite: *the idea is the easy part!* You can have a brilliant innovation that leads to an unsustainable business or a boring, commonplace idea that drives a fantastic business. Much of this book will be about all the factors *other than your idea* that will make or break your startup, and all the essential questions and challenges that first-time entrepreneurs tend to overlook.

New entrepreneurs usually equate the value of a startup with the "wow factor" of its innovation. It's true that some massively successful startups, such as Tesla and Google, were founded on genuinely significant technological breakthroughs, but those are a small minority, and even they didn't get to where they are on the power of the idea alone. They just happen to get the lion's share of media coverage and public adulation.

The majority of successful startups, in contrast, integrate previously existing ideas in new ways rather than inventing something utterly original. It's an approach I call "some assembly required," as you'll see in the chapter on choosing opportunities. Often, a relatively small twist on a previously existing business model can lead to big success. For instance, Facebook wasn't the first social-media platform, but it was the first that required users to use their real identity, which changed the experience.

Instagram wasn't the first service for sharing photos online, but it was the first to offer filters and make sharing fun and social. Dollar Shave Club became a billion-dollar business without a single technological breakthrough. And what was Starbucks at first but a chain of expensive coffee shops that didn't offer table service but introduced exotic (at the time) espressos and lattes?

One of my favorite examples is Zappos, the online shoe retailer. Not only did founder Tony Hsieh not have a great idea—he didn't even have a *good* idea! Letting customers order five pairs of shoes, try them on at home, and then ship back four of them for free? Those high costs made the business model terrible, and despite strong growth, the company was barely profitable before it was acquired by Amazon.

Sometimes breakthrough ideas can even have a negative impact. One company that we started and funded at Domain used a cutting-edge technology to insert human genes into mice. That was a real innovation, and we were smitten by the science, but we searched in vain for a viable business to apply it. We tried to develop a testing laboratory for new products that used "humanized mice," but it didn't get off the ground because the current methods of animal testing were too entrenched. We then pivoted to trying to use the technology to grow new organs. That also didn't work—too many differences between mice and men.

Beyond your idea, the team you hire and manage will also be a make-or-break factor in your startup's success. So will your effectiveness at raising capital and executing through tough challenges, as we'll see in the chapters ahead. A great way to lose money is to say, "This idea is so good that even with idiots in charge, we can't possibly lose money."

WHY SHOULD YOU LISTEN TO ME?

This book isn't a memoir, but knowing my background will help you see why I'm neither a rah-rah cheerleader nor a Debbie Downer about entrepreneurship. So here's the short version of my long and winding road, which has been filled with at least as many flops as successes. I'm actually proud of those flops, along with the more than forty successful companies I've helped launch and the tens of thousands of jobs I've helped create. Startups are a game of home runs and strikeouts, and it's no coincidence that the best home-run hitters of all time also struck out more than their peers.

My first job after college was with a management training program at New York Telephone. They started me in sales, pitching phone services to small businesses. I sold the first electronic switchboard in New York City, but it didn't work well. We made multiple unsuccessful attempts to fix the problem, sending out a supervisor, then a manager, then the head of engineering. I'll never forget the next call I got from the customer: "Mr. Dovey, you keep sending out people with nicer and nicer suits who know less and less." That was a good lesson in separating competence from job title.

A week later he called back to ask what I was doing for lunch. When I said I was free, he replied, "Great, come to the corner of 7th Avenue and 14th Street, so you can catch this thing when I throw it out the window!" We eventually did repair that switchboard, but it was a harrowing few weeks.

I wasn't a natural salesperson, but I got good enough to get promoted to sales manager. While still in my early twenties, I was managing seven sales reps in their thirties and forties and earning enough to get married, buy a house, and start a family. But I started to get bored and restless. One of my mentors had gone to Harvard Business School and made it sound exciting. But it was scary to give up job security and a good salary for an unknowable future. I'll never forget asking my grandmother, an English immigrant with a Cockney accent, for her opinion. As I showed her my carefully written list of the pros and cons of business school, she looked me in the eye. "Forget about that list. If you don't do it, will you be kicking yourself in the arse in ten years?"

A few years later, MBA in hand, I landed at Howmet, a fast-growing manufacturer of sophisticated metals, which was more exciting than the phone company. I gravitated to the medical-products side of the business—artificial hips, knees, dental implants, and so on. Within two years, I was running my first business unit and loving the fact that I'd get credit for its success or blame for its failure. I had a great boss who gave me a lot of latitude.

One of our customers was Survival Technology Inc. (STI), a startup founded by a distinguished cardiovascular researcher named Stanley Sarnoff. He had invented an automatic syringe system that could make it easier to save patients who were having a heart attack. STI was a side project for him, an attempt to commercialize his invention. But he knew nothing about running a startup, so he hired me to run it for him. I wasn't restless at Howmet, but the STI opportunity was too exciting to pass up.

At first, STI was just two engineers, an accountant, an office manager, and me. That startup became my life for the next ten years, as it grew to become one of the ten fastest-growing companies tracked by *Inc.* magazine. Dr. Sarnoff's auto-injector technology, originally designed for heart attack patients, evolved into the EpiPen, which has saved countless lives as an emergency treatment for allergic reactions.[*]

THE GRASS IS ALWAYS GREENER IN A FORTUNE 500 BOARDROOM

Though I loved STI, I still thought often about what it would be like to run a Fortune 500 company, perhaps as a side effect of Harvard's snobbery toward startups. So I got excited when I was recruited to become president of the medical-devices division of Rorer, then a leading pharmaceutical and medical-device company. About a year later, I was promoted to EVP for all of Rorer's strategic planning, plus pharmaceutical R&D, while still running

---

[*] You'll hear more about my experiences at STI, including the birth of the EpiPen, in the chapters ahead.

my own division. They were setting me up to become the next president and COO to support a new CEO.

During my three years as president of Rorer, I was responsible for streamlining it by making deals to buy and sell product lines and entire units. I also helped the company shake off the mentality that we were just trying to do the same stuff better, not anything new.*

On the downside, corporate-office politics started wearing me down. For instance, one evening I was on the phone with the head of our German operation, dealing with a serious manufacturing problem, when our CFO barged in, insisting he had to speak with me. I waved him into my office and braced for whatever financial issue required my immediate attention. His "urgent problem" was that our VP of human resources had a better parking spot than he did. I was too stunned to reply.

My assumption had once been that if you climb high enough in a big organization, you can escape office politics. The reality is that you not only can't escape it; you're expected to help maintain it. I found myself spending countless hours settling debates about the cafeteria's paint colors or how much snow justified declaring a snow day. My attempts to say, "Who cares, let's focus on what's important" were not appreciated.

The final episode that pushed me over the edge was a lengthy meeting with thirteen top-level executives on the crucial issue of . . . the Christmas party. Should it be paid for by employees, the

---

* You'll also hear more about Rorer in the chapters ahead.

company, or a combination of the two? I thought it was obvious that we should expense it and that the question barely required thirty seconds of thought. But after more than an hour of debate, when we still couldn't reach consensus, our CEO called for a vote. When it came around the table to me, I couldn't contain my frustration: "Am I allowed to not give a shit?"

Like many people, I didn't realize how unhappy I was about my job, and I needed someone else to recognize the signs of burnout. Luckily, my wife noticed. I finally had to agree one morning, when she pointed out that I'd hit the snooze bar on my alarm five times before finally dragging myself out of bed.

So many people I would later meet in the startup world are refugees from the corporate world. They all say something like, "I wish I had made the jump sooner." On balance, Rorer was a great experience, a chance to apply my entrepreneurial skills to make some real changes in a large company environment. But now it was time for a new challenge.

VENTURE CAPITAL: EVOLVING FROM QUARTERBACK TO COACH

One of my venture-capitalist friends offered to let me shadow him for a week, and I was immediately excited by the prospect of becoming a VC. At the time, I didn't know much about them, just that VCs raised money from institutions like pension plans and university endowments to invest in and guide startups. The role appealed to me because it would give me an opportunity to work with a variety of companies at the same time, sharing my insights as a coach rather than carrying out the plays as a quarterback. An introduction led me to Jim Blair, and I agreed to join his new firm, Domain Associates, just as they were raising their first $40 million fund. Three decades later, Domain has raised ten such funds—a total of more than $2.8 billion to finance the dreams of hundreds of entrepreneurs.

Venture capital turned out to be my true calling, as well as a never-ending education in what does and doesn't work for startups. I started to develop useful rules of thumb about industries, founders, products, leadership strategies, and financial metrics. I also learned the hard way that every rule of thumb has exceptions, because every startup is unique for one reason or another. Those exceptions have kept me humble and will hopefully help you resist any temptation toward overconfidence. Startups are the ultimate "it depends" endeavor; you never know anything with 100 percent certainty.

For instance, I used to tell my colleagues at Domain that we should never invest in laser-technology startups because Rorer had failed with several laser-based products. They cost a ton of money to develop but always had problems that prevented mass adoption. But then we got pitched on an ophthalmology laser product by an entrepreneur I had previously worked with at Rorer. I almost rejected it out of hand without even reading the full business plan. But then I had second thoughts. I knew that this entrepreneur was smart and competent, and he was aware of those failed laser products at Rorer. If he was willing to pitch Domain, he must have found a way to make sure his product would work. Sure enough, our due diligence showed that he had something special. We invested and did very well with it.

A ROAD MAP FOR THIS BOOK

I've organized the chapters ahead around the six key aspects of a founder's entrepreneurial journey, all of which can confound first-timers, or even fifth-timers.

- Deciding whether or not you want to try your hand at a startup, based on your unique combination of background, skills, personality, and other factors (chapter two).
- Choosing business opportunities that will give your startup at least a fighting shot at enduring profitability (chapter three).
- Figuring out how, when, and why to pitch venture capitalists or other institutional investors, based on how *they* will be looking at *you* (chapter four).
- Hiring and leading a team that will enable your startup to thrive and building a workplace culture that will make them want to stay (chapter five).
- Executing for growth by focusing on what's truly important, solving thorny problems, and pivoting when necessary (chapter six).
- Planning ahead for various possible outcomes, from an IPO to a private sale to bankruptcy, as well the possibility that you'll be asked to leave (chapter seven).

Throughout, I'll debunk common myths and share true stories that haven't already been covered in hundreds of previous books. Instead of rehashing legends like the waffle iron that launched Nike or the door that Jeff Bezos used as a desk, I'll explore equally fascinating startups in the natural sciences, medicine, and biotechnology that rarely get much attention. Some will be from medium-sized or even large companies because I believe entrepreneurs can learn essential lessons from the smart and foolish moves of organizations of all sizes. The startup mindset doesn't have to vanish when you reach a certain size, and we can learn a lot from corporate leaders who never lose their hunger for disruption and reinvention.

I should warn you what you *won't* be getting. This is not an encyclopedic guide to every possible question an entrepreneur might ask, down to advice on how to deduct your home office on your tax returns. If you want that level of minutia, you might seek out one of those reference-style guidebooks that can double as a doorstop. Instead, I'm aiming for the bigger picture: helping you decide if entrepreneurship is the right path for you, then preparing you for the inevitable challenges and frustrations that will arise if you begin this journey. You can still expect to make some mistakes, but at least they will be your own, *new* mistakes—not the ones that I and many of my fellow entrepreneurs have already made. (I'll disclose plenty of those—reluctantly!)

THE THRILL RIDE OF A GREAT STARTUP

Despite all these caveats and warnings, I want to stress that a great startup is more exciting than your favorite roller coaster or a trip to Las Vegas. It's more intellectually challenging—in a good way—than any test you took in school. It's more emotional than any high-stakes sporting event you've ever played in or watched.

To give you a taste of what I mean, here's the story (or at least the beginning of the story) of one of my favorite startup investments ever. For context, keep in mind that in a typical year I receive about 1,500 startup proposals, listen to fifty pitches, drill down on fifteen or twenty of them, and close five to seven deals. So each deal is a huge gamble, not merely of money but also of time and energy and opportunity cost.

In early 1998, I was approached by a fellow VC, Joe Lacob of Kleiner Perkins, who had just invested in an early-stage orthodontics startup with a radically new concept for braces. He told me that Align Technology had been founded by two newly minted Stanford MBAs, Zia Chishti and Kelsey Wirth, who were also in a romantic relationship. In just this brief exchange, I spotted three red flags. First, the entrepreneurs were inexperienced. Second, the dental industry was conservative and hard for newcomers to break into. Third, a startup run by a couple could face trouble if they broke up. My rules of thumb were all saying "pass."

But a closer look revealed that Align had a potentially huge idea buried in its badly written proposal. Clear plastic aligners that were virtually invisible—hence the product name "Invisalign"—would obviously have more appeal than metal braces did. They could be removed instantly for meals and social occasions, making them ideal for adults as well as kids. The market for adult orthodonture was still virtually untapped—and enormous! And Align owned patents for the whole concept of removable aligners, without regard to specific production methods.

I still had four big questions, however. Did the product really work as well as they claimed? How did patients feel about it? What did orthodontists think? (You can't sell medical devices without enthusiastic medical professionals.) And could Invisalign braces be produced at a reasonable cost to keep the price viable for a mass market?

Several orthodontists I reached out to thought Invisalign wouldn't work. Later, I learned that other VCs had also found resistance from orthodontists. The company's engineering studies said otherwise, however, so I began to suspect that these orthodontists were biased because Invisalign threatened their existing business model and professional training. Every new idea has to overcome the resistance of whoever stands to lose from it.

With their "if it ain't broke, don't fix it" attitude, these orthodontists reminded me of the orthopedic surgeons who initially opposed arthroscopic surgery when I was involved in its introduction at Rorer. Unlike highly invasive traditional surgery, arthroscopic technology allows surgeons to manipulate instruments through small holes, using a video monitor. Most skeptics came around when the benefits of this new tech became undeniable. I had a hunch that once data proved the appeal of Invisalign, most orthodontists would see an opportunity to add adult patients without losing their young ones.

We set up focus groups to interview potential consumers, whose enthusiasm was the opposite of the negativity among orthodontists. Even when I probed about price sensitivity, many said they would pay tens of thousands of dollars for a nice smile that didn't require years of embarrassing, inconvenient braces.

The evidence was still unclear as to whether Invisalign could be manufactured cost-effectively. That would remain a mystery until the company started to scale up, so I had to accept a level of uncertainty about this part of Align's business model.

Finally, I interviewed the founders. Despite their lack of experience, I found them totally committed and hardworking. I asked a question that other potential investors had politely avoided: What would happen to Align if they ever broke up as a couple? They had given this a lot of thought and replied that if their personal lives ever interfered with the business, one of them would leave the company. That was the no-drama response I'd hoped for.

Putting everything together, I was in; Domain made a significant investment in Align. The technology was appealing to consumers and protected by patents. Even if manufacturing costs ended up higher than we hoped, the focus groups told me there would still be a market willing to pay premium prices.

A great idea, solid financial prospects, enthusiastic consumers—sounds like a slam dunk, right? Not even close. As you will see later in the book, Align faced many execution challenges on its eventual road to success, including the departures of the founders and several operating problems that almost put the company out of business.

The point of this story isn't that I was brilliant to make that investment. Of those five to seven deals I commit to every year, a few usually turn out to be busts, and I've lost count of all the great opportunities that I foolishly turned down. My point, rather, is that startups are never straightforward, even when they appear from a distance to be runaway successes. That's what makes them exciting and deeply satisfying when they finally work.

Align's eventual success depended not on a single big idea—as great as that idea was—but on countless decisions made on the fly and the leadership team's ability to focus, pivot, adapt to unforeseen problems, and execute on their constantly evolving strategy. In other words, *the idea was the easy part*.

Howard Stevenson, a professor at Harvard Business School, may have come up with the best definition of entrepreneurship in the fewest possible words: "the pursuit of opportunity beyond resources controlled."[1] I love this definition because it captures an inventive mindset that spots new opportunities and then assembles the resources needed to make the most of them. To me, this process is endlessly fascinating. Turn the page, and let's start exploring it.

2

GOING FOR IT
Do You Have What It Takes to Be a Successful Entrepreneur?

This chapter will help you figure out if entrepreneurship makes sense for you, based on current realities rather than outdated myths about who is actually qualified to launch a startup effectively. Those myths often discourage people who might contribute fresh perspectives that we urgently need in new startups. Fortunately, there are now significantly more opportunities for women, people of color, and others who defy the "startup bro" stereotypes in one way or another.

Despite these opportunities, it's still not true that absolutely everyone can or should be an entrepreneur. So, before we explore the demographics, backgrounds, and personality traits of people who might become great entrepreneurs, let's start with some valid reasons why you might want to put this book down and try something else.

WHAT DOES A FOUNDER *NOT* LOOK LIKE?

In my experience, people with certain tendencies and beliefs tend to do poorly at launching and running startups. These include:

- Anyone overwhelmingly focused on making money rather than building something great, serving customers, changing an industry, or other, nobler goals.
- Anyone who doesn't want to work hard or who assumes that success will come easily if they have a good idea and delegate all the messy parts, perhaps even while working a different full-time job.
- Anyone prone to distraction instead of identifying and focusing on what's truly important. Distractions will be coming at you constantly!
- Anyone too stubborn to pivot on strategy and tactics when a plan just isn't working.
- Anyone who can't tolerate ambiguity or messiness or can't make decisions with partial information. For most of the

questions you'll face, the answer will be, "It depends." And no one will give you a gold star for neatness.

- Anyone in a rush to cash out. You have to be prepared to stick it out for five to seven years, maybe longer. One startup I know assumed a six-month exit—more than ten years ago!
- Anyone prone to perfectionism. Very often, anything worth doing will be worth doing poorly. Your path to success will be very wobbly, never perfectly straight.
- Anyone who wants their company to stay small forever. Great founders aspire to scale, even when they still have minimal cash, staff, or infrastructure.

If you see yourself somewhere in this list, you should probably move on to some other plan. If not, let's look at why you almost certainly *do* have the potential to become a successful entrepreneur.

WHAT DOES A FOUNDER LOOK LIKE?

When you hear the term "startup founder," do you automatically picture someone white, male, young, based in Silicon Valley, and with a STEM or business degree from an elite university? While there are still plenty of founders who fit those stereotypes, they are becoming less common all the time.

Here's a summary chart I often share with audiences about the gaps between common perceptions and realities about successful founders:

FACTOR	PERCEPTION	REALITY
Education	Elite	Wide range
Ethnicity	White	Increasingly diverse
Gender	Men	Increasingly women
Age	Under 35	Wide range
Motivation	Money/power/ego	Often passion or mission
Expertise	Tech expert	Often a generalist
Personality	Extroverts	Wide range
Risk appetite	Risk driven	Risk averse/opportunity driven

Let's explore these shifts and some examples of people who are redefining what a "typical" entrepreneur looks like.

EDUCATION: EMBRACING THE SCHOOL OF HARD KNOCKS

Many founders still major in business, economics, or one of the STEM fields, often at elite universities like Stanford, MIT, or the Ivies. This leads many aspiring entrepreneurs to assume that they have to do likewise. But I've found zero correlation between the subjects you study, where you study them, and how well or poorly you'll do at a startup. Over the years, I've funded great startups led by people who majored in various liberal arts, including a music major who now runs a sophisticated medical-device company. I've even funded entrepreneurs who never went to college at all. According to Forbes, among the four hundred richest people in the United States in 2012:

- Twenty-nine had master of science degrees.[1]
- Thirty-five had law degrees.[2]
- Sixty-three had only high school degrees.[3]
- Most of the rest simply had a BA or BS from a non-elite college.

Some of the many high school or college dropouts who became billionaires by founding or building new companies include Evan Williams of Twitter, Larry Ellison of Oracle, John Mackey of Whole Foods, Paul Allen of Microsoft, Hiroshi Yamauchi of Nintendo, and Walt Disney of, well, you know.

Mary Fisher might be my favorite example that proves a lack of business or technical education is no handicap. She's an artist who never went to college, but she became one of the most effective biotech entrepreneurs I've ever worked with.

In her early twenties, Mary took a corporate job to pay the bills while she tried to make it as an artist. To her own surprise, she found that she had a talent for making things happen in business. One job led to another, including management roles. Mary realized that she was better at bringing people together, inspiring them, and changing the world through biotech and pharmaceuticals than she was at creating art.

After senior positions at Cephalon and Acorda Therapeutics, she became CEO of SkinMedica, a pioneer in dermatology. SkinMedica was later sold to Allergan, the inventor and maker of Botox, where it has continued to thrive as an important product line. Mary went on to launch a couple of dermatology startups that were funded by Domain, including Colorescience, where she is currently chair and CEO. Their key product, Sunforgettable, has been hailed as one of the best sunscreens on the market, in part because it doesn't contain any chemicals that are harmful to the skin.

How did Mary build such an impressive career without a college diploma, especially in a high-tech sector driven by cutting-edge science? She didn't need to be able to understand the science of artificial skin or premium-quality sunscreen. Instead, she needed to integrate information and inspire teams. She gathers disparate pieces of knowledge and expertise from many different areas and combines them in new ways to generate new product ideas. Her ability to integrate information leads to strategies no one else has considered, including experts on her staff who have advanced degrees.

Mary also has outstanding interpersonal skills, which have enabled her to recruit, retain, and motivate outstanding teams at each of her companies. As an entrepreneur, you don't necessarily need to master the technical details of your product. But you definitely need to recognize which information is important and which is secondary or irrelevant. And you need to be able to inspire your people to trust your insights and embrace your vision for the company.

We often see liberal-arts majors thrive at tech companies because the tech is ultimately just a small part of the overall picture.

ETHNICITY: DIVERSITY IMPROVES RESULTS

The tradition that entrepreneurs are overwhelmingly white is changing more slowly than I'd like to see. According to Crunchbase, in 2019 just 1 percent of VC-backed founders were Black; only 1.8 percent were Latino, and only 2.8 percent were of Middle Eastern heritage.[4]

Getting funding can be especially tough for Black entrepreneurs. In 2016, the Center for Global Policy Solutions reported that "due to discriminatory financing practices and a bias towards . . . white males, America is losing out on over 1.1 million minority-owned businesses. As a result, the economy is foregoing over nine million potential jobs and $300 billion in collective national income."[5]

Many organizations finally recognize this problem and are actively trying to solve it. For instance, in 2021 Goldman Sachs set up a new investment initiative of $10 billion in direct-investment capital and $100 million in philanthropic capital over the next decade. The initiative, One Million Black Women, was designed to support startups by at least a million Black and female entrepreneurs by 2030.[6] Many other organizations have also been created to support minority-group entrepreneurs, including Techstars, Backstage Capital, and Opportunity Hub at SXSW.[7]

There are definite signs of progress. For instance, Black women represented 42 percent of new women-owned businesses in 2019—three times their share of the female population—and 36 percent of all Black-owned employer businesses.[8] Sixty-four percent of new women-owned businesses were started by women of color in 2020, and there was an 87 percent increase in the number of Latina-owned businesses.[9]

Research suggests that ethnically diverse work teams get better results. For instance, by analyzing a data set of startups that participated in the Techstars accelerator program between 2007 and 2018, one study found that a startup team's ethnic diversity is positively associated with the amount of investment capital raised,[10] suggesting that diversity really is a business advantage, not just a moral imperative.

One Black entrepreneur I greatly admire is my friend Stanley Lewis, an MD who has started two successful biotech companies so far. His first, Eselle Health, pioneered a hormone delivery technology for treating the complications of diabetes and other metabolic disorders. His second, A28 Therapeutics, is focusing on targeted treatments for cancers that manifest themselves in the liver, one of the most deadly and frustrating branches of oncology. Stanley is exceptional in several ways. Like many entrepreneurs, he's a generalist who looks at challenges from a broad perspective, yet he can also deploy his medical expertise to drive impressive innovations.

He grew up in an East Texas town of about twenty thousand people, where he was valedictorian of his high school class—a true accomplishment for a Black student in that mostly white environment. He went to the University of Texas for both his undergraduate and medical degrees, despite having been accepted at premier universities across the country; top-tier private schools would have been too expensive, even with financial aid. As he established his stellar medical career, he never showed an interest in entrepreneurship. But as many of us have experienced, one moment of serendipity changed his path.

Stanley was teaching at the University of Texas's medical school when he was approached by an entrepreneur who wanted to hire him as the director of drug development for her startup. He felt a kinship with this Chinese American woman, since they both sometimes felt like outsiders in biotech. He also remembered that his father often emphasized how great it was to work for yourself. So Stanley left his secure position at UT to try life at a startup. He liked it so much that after that company was sold, he started one of his own.

I asked him what it was like to be a Black entrepreneur—an advantage, a disadvantage, or neither? He indicated that it was all three at different times. For instance, when he first moved to San Diego to join its growing biotech hub, he was invited to a high-profile conference for entrepreneurs, executives, and venture capitalists. He was surprised to see that he had been assigned to the VIP table for the first session, an honor he attributes to the industry's desire to celebrate diversity. But during the networking/

social event that evening, he and his business partner split up to work opposite halves of the large room. His partner, who was white, had no problem talking to people about their new company; he came back with about twenty business cards. Stanley, on the other hand, found people reluctant to approach him or engage in conversation. He ended the night with only two business cards.

Stanley believes that diversity has greatly improved since he first went into entrepreneurship, but true inclusion—genuinely welcoming people from all backgrounds—still hasn't caught up. It's essential that startups bring diverse perspectives to bear on whatever challenges they are trying to solve. For instance, Stanley noted that experts from the Black community were essentially left out of the conversation about how to improve COVID-19 vaccination rates within the Black community. Situations like that hurt everyone, not merely the groups that are discriminated against.

GENDER: PROGRESS TOWARD EQUALITY

First the bad news about progress toward gender equality: women-led startups received just 2.3 percent of VC funding in 2020.[11] Now the good news: as of December 2020, there are 114 percent more women entrepreneurs than there were twenty years ago, and 40 percent of all US businesses are now women-owned.[12]

More good news: women aren't merely participating in entrepreneurship; they are thriving. Private tech companies led by women average 35 percent higher ROI. Women-founded companies in First Round Capital's portfolio outperformed companies founded by men by 63 percent. Furthermore, according to a 2019 survey of women in technology leadership, 28 percent of start-ups have at least one female cofounder; 40 percent have at least one woman on their board; and 56 percent now have at least one woman in an executive position.[13] These kinds of numbers make me optimistic about continued progress toward equality.

One of many wonderful female entrepreneurs I've worked with is Bonnie Anderson, an award-winning, forty-year veteran of the life-sciences sector. She's the cofounder and former CEO (now executive chairwoman) of Veracyte, a diagnostics company that launched in 2008 and went public in 2013. Its initial focus was improving the way thyroid cancer was diagnosed. For years, when people showed symptoms of thyroid cancer, the standard test led to a lot of false positives or ambiguous results. Conservative oncologists ordered thyroid surgery for many patients who didn't really need it, which led to negative consequences for those patients. Bonnie's team figured out a diagnostic process that greatly increased the accuracy of thyroid-cancer testing, which greatly reduced unnecessary surgery. They eliminated a lot of human suffering.

When she first came to Domain to pitch Veracyte, I was struck by Bonnie's passion and deep sense of purpose. She had attended a modest school, Indiana University of Pennsylvania. She was a great listener, able to assimilate a ton of information to figure out how to position and market her company. She understood that you can't try to be all things to all people, because overreaching will kill a startup. Veracyte focused on doing the best possible thyroid testing to drive therapeutic decision-making before expanding into other kinds of testing. The company became a resounding success, with Bonnie not only effectively implementing the thyroid test but also developing other tests that were highly effective and cost-saving.

AGE: LIKE A FINE WINE

Successful founders in their twenties get lots of press coverage, but they are the exception.

According to the Kauffman Foundation, the average age of successful tech company founders is thirty-nine, and twice as many US-born tech entrepreneurs start ventures in their fifties as do those in their early twenties. In 2018, the highest rates of entrepreneurial activity occurred among the 45–54 and 55–64 age cohorts. The group with the lowest activity was those aged 20–34.[14] Also as of 2018, adults between fifty-five and sixty-four made up 25.8 percent of new entrepreneurs, a significant increase over the 14.8 percent they represented in 1996. Seventy-five percent of founders have more than six years of experience in their industry, and half have more than ten years.[15]

Research presented in the *Harvard Business Review* notes: "The average age of high-tech founders falls in the early forties . . . Our evidence points to entrepreneurial performance rising sharply with age before cresting in the late fifties . . . Relative to founders with no relevant experience, those with at least three years of prior work experience in the same narrow industry as their startup were

85 percent more likely to launch a highly successful startup."[16] A Founder Institute study agreed that "an older age is actually a better predictor of entrepreneurial success."[17] Some notable people who became successful entrepreneurs for the first time in middle age or beyond include Cheryl Kellond of Bia Sport (43), Linda Avey of 23andMe (46), Jim Kimsey of AOL (46), Joseph Lubin of Ethereum (50), and Tom Siebel of C3 (55).[18]

Many companies still have a mandatory retirement age of sixty-five or even younger, a relic of a bygone age when no one was expected to accomplish much after their mid-sixties. But these days, it seems like half the people running the business world and the government are over seventy. Maybe sixty really is the new forty? These mandatory retirement policies accidentally create a large pool of experienced, highly knowledgeable people who are forced to leave jobs they still excel at. What a waste of great talent by corporate America! I've seen several of these retirees get snapped up by startups and, in some cases, launch their own companies.

For instance, in late 2000, three young entrepreneurs presented Domain with an idea to start a new pharmaceutical company based on revitalizing existing products that had been pushed to the wayside by the major drug companies.* Domain loved their business plan but not their inexperience. So we suggested that they bump up one of their consultants and board members, John Spitznagel, to CEO. John was a veteran pharmaceutical executive

---

* We'll return to this startup, ESP, in more detail in chapters five and six.

for Johnson & Johnson who had run a large sales force of 1,000+ and had previously been CEO of two midsized companies. But now he was available, thanks to a forced retirement.

Making him CEO was somewhat risky because John had never been involved in a startup before, and I'm sure he also thought it was a personal risk. But he loved being a first-time entrepreneur in his sixties, and he was great at it. That startup earned back ten times our investment, and after it was sold, John went on to launch two more companies. People like John have the experience and desire to make things happen, and they don't need on-the-job training. If you ever have an opportunity to recruit a retiree for your team, give it serious consideration! Or if you are a retiree yourself, consider launching a startup of your own.

MOTIVATION: PASSION OVER PROFIT

The stereotypical "startup bro" is motivated by a bottomless hunger for money, power, acclaim, attention, and ego reinforcement. In reality, the greedy, ego-driven founder is a rarity. The majority, including the most successful in particular, are primarily motivated by mission and passion, not money. They want to build a great company and improve the lives of their customers. If they can get rich in the process, that's great, but for most of them it's not the core goal.

More than likely, your excitement about your work comes from your sense of purpose. Very few people would be willing to double their income by signing a five-year contract to dig a hole every morning and fill it every afternoon. If that's true for salaried workers, it's even more true for entrepreneurs, who are more likely to be motivated by purpose because their financial outcome is completely uncertain. Focusing on money doesn't give anyone peace of mind, freedom, or a feeling of success.

Naval Ravikant of AngelList (nicknamed the Buddha of Silicon Valley) is all about love and connection. Jack Dorsey, the CEO of Square, is a low-key vegan hippie who was criticized for not ruthlessly monetizing Twitter while he was its CEO.

A great example of a startup founder with noble motivations is Harith Rajagopalan, the cofounder and CEO of Fractyl Health. I've been lucky to be part of building this exciting new company for over ten years as an investor and board member. Harith has both an MD and a PhD from Johns Hopkins, and spent years as a successful cardiologist and scientist. He did groundbreaking, award-winning research on intestinal cancers that was published in top medical journals such as *Nature* and *Science*. He later completed a research fellowship at the Harvard Stem Cell Institute at Harvard Medical School.

Why did Harith pivot from that amazing research career to pursue entrepreneurship? Not for fame or fortune, but to help as many people as possible by turning his research into commercially viable products. Fractyl Health develops "organ-editing metabolic therapeutics" as a pioneering new approach to the treatment of type 2 diabetes (T2D). In simple terms, the technology has the promise of curing type 2 diabetes, unlike the more than forty medications that just treat the symptoms. Harith believes that

Fractyl's treatments for gut health may eventually lead to many other breakthroughs beyond T2D.

Harith has proven to be as good a CEO as he is a doctor and scientist. He blends his technical expertise with an intuitive feel for recruiting and inspiring that mission-driven team full of innovators. It's clear to everyone who deals with Fractyl that they aren't in it for money or ego but rather to help millions of patients. Harith combines sky-high ambition for his company with deep personal humility. He never brags about his credentials or honors. He's a great listener who clearly respects all of his colleagues and wants to hear from them. He knows that he doesn't know everything, so he keeps an open mind. I've watched him in board meetings, intensely focused on whoever is talking, taking notes so he can continue learning. That combination makes him a very effective startup leader—the opposite of the stereotype on so many levels.

EXPERTISE: DON'T TRY TO BE A JACK OF ALL TRADES

Another myth that deters potential entrepreneurs is that you need to be great at every key business skill. It sometimes seems like the ones who get all the attention are simultaneously experts at technology, finance, leadership, strategic planning, marketing, and operations management. No wonder new founders can feel intimidated!

In reality, most successful entrepreneurs excel at two or three key skills and delegate the rest. They have clarity about their own strengths and weaknesses, as well as the humility to let other people take responsibility for functional roles that don't play to their strengths. For instance, if you're terrible at budgeting or sales, don't let that deter you. If your startup is sound, you'll be able to recruit others to take responsibility for those or other areas. Many of the best founders rely on colleagues who compensate for skills they lack.

A classic example is Steve Jobs, master of user experience, who knew relatively little about how Apple's technology worked. Even in the early days of Apple, he knew almost nothing about its products. But he was outstanding at hiring and motivating talent, and he had an intuitive genius for marketing innovative products.

I think one notable exception to this principle is storytelling. The ability to articulate your vision for your company is so central that you do need a minimal standard of competence in delivering narrative-driven presentations. Research has found that entrepreneurs who master storytelling are consistently more successful. You can't simply explain how a piece of technology works; you have to build a narrative about why it works and what can be done with it. I can't count the number of bad pitches I've sat through—slide after slide of data and graphs, with no context or narrative. I try to focus on the substance and ignore the style, but it's difficult.

I vividly remember one meeting during which a founder showed slide after slide about mouse experiments and different doses of chemicals attacking specific cell types with exotic names. But he never even mentioned that he was trying to cure cancer!

Did he think that would be boring? In those situations, a VC is likely thinking (if not screaming), "So what? What can we do with it?!" The answers to every other question can wait.*

As consultant Martin Zwilling puts it, "The entrepreneur's challenge is to effectively communicate their value proposition, not only to customers, but also to vendors, partners, investors, and their own team. . . . facts only go so far. Stories often work better, because humans don't always make rational decisions. Most people care the most about the things that touch, move, and inspire them. They make decisions based on emotion, and then look for the facts that support these decisions. Thus it behooves every entrepreneur to learn how to craft stories from their personal experience and the world at large that make an emotional connection, as well as tie in the facts."[19]

While storytelling comes naturally to some people, for others it is a learned skill. I have seen the least verbally oriented scientists and engineers take courses in speaking skills to help them improve at sharing their visions. Others work one-on-one with a freelance speaking coach and practice until they get better. There's no shame in taking advantage of that kind of help, because it will really pay off—not in some mythical sixty-second elevator pitch

---

* We'll return to what VCs are thinking about your pitch in chapter four.

but in the ability to hold people's attention for a half hour or more and make a real impact on their thinking.*

A great example of essential versus nonessential skills is Cam Garner, a prominent member of the San Diego biotech community. Even though he took chemistry and biology in college and worked briefly as a lab tech, he has no real medical or technical background to rely on. Instead, he has an uncanny knack for leading successful startups by focusing on his strengths and delegating the rest.

I met Cam when he was running marketing for a biotech startup called Hybritech, whose CEO was my friend and business-school classmate Ted Greene. In 1986, they were making impressive progress on monoclonal antibodies, which led to a generous buyout offer from Eli Lilly, the Big Pharma giant. Lilly asked the Hybritech management team to relocate to Lilly's headquarters in Indianapolis, but that held no appeal for Ted, Cam, and their colleagues. So after they sold the company, they went their separate ways to pursue new startup ideas in San Diego. Hybritech was the big bang that unleashed an astonishing range of new biotech companies in that city.

Cam founded or cofounded more than a dozen companies in the decades after the Hybritech sale, and the overwhelming majority successfully went public or were bought by bigger

---

* We'll return to storytelling in chapter four, about the art of getting funding.

companies. They included Dura Pharmaceuticals, Cadence Pharmaceuticals, Xcel Pharmaceuticals, and Zavante Therapeutics. With that track record, his successes clearly weren't just luck. How did he run all those science-driven companies without any kind of science background?

Cam is the first to admit that he's not a scientific visionary—he's a skilled spotter and manager of other people's visions. He's great at sorting through information, spotting what's important, hiring great teams, and managing organizations. If you come to him with a vision, he can help you execute it to its highest potential. I think of his talent as almost like that of a record producer. George Martin didn't write the Beatles's songs, or play their instruments, or come up with their cutting-edge ideas. But he was essential in turning those raw ideas into brilliant records.

When I asked Cam to share his best advice for entrepreneurs, he replied:

- Figure out what matters and focus on it.
- Get comfortable with chaos and ambiguity.
- Keep an even keel when things are going poorly.
- Trust your ability to work your way out of a jam by focusing on the next step.
- Listen to others, but be prepared to make decisions without all the facts.
- Understand your shortcomings so you can hire people who fill in your gaps.

- Be candid with employees regarding the status of the company.
- Communicate regularly about strategy, results, and challenges.
- Stay connected with all of your constituents—board, investors, employees.
- Delegate and monitor—both are equally essential.

Please note that nothing on that list says, "Have a brilliant vision for new products" or "Master the technology of your industry" or "Prove that you're the smartest one in the room."

PERSONALITY: STAY TRUE TO YOUR OWN STYLE

Another common myth is that you have to be an extrovert to succeed as an entrepreneur. Many assume that they have to love networking and hold the attention of everyone at a presentation with the power of their charisma. But after working with hundreds of entrepreneurs, I've found that classic extroverts are extremely rare. The essential trait isn't extroversion; it's the ability to absorb and integrate disparate and sometimes conflicting information to make decisions. Listening is a far more valuable skill than talking! Introverts can learn how to articulate their goals with enough clarity and passion that others will be eager to join the enterprise.

Social scientists have searched in vain for any consistent correlation between entrepreneurs and personality traits.[20] Many iconic entrepreneurs are introverts, including Bill Gates, Steve Wozniak, Mark Zuckerberg, Larry Page, and Warren Buffett. That hasn't stopped them from honing their leadership, problem-solving, and decision-making skills. One study spent ten years examining the personalities of two thousand CEOs and concluded that the majority of the successful ones were introverts.[21] Even Elon Musk once said, "I'm basically like an introverted engineer, so, it took a lot of practice and effort to be able to go up on stage and not just stammer basically . . . as the CEO, you kind of have to."[22]

The common perception that introversion is a barrier to leadership can lead to prejudicial hiring practices. For example, a UK study found that highly extroverted people had a much higher chance of landing a higher-earning job.[23] But while extroverts may get hired more easily, there's a case to be made that introverts often make better leaders. They tend to be above-average listeners and observers, which can help them develop stronger relationships with their teams.

David Hale, another key player in the San Diego biotech community, is one of the most introverted, soft-spoken, and circumspect entrepreneurs I've ever worked with. He started as an executive at Johnson & Johnson in Baltimore and might have stayed in corporate America if not for one fluke moment. One March day, after ignoring repeated overtures from a tech recruiter, he picked up his own phone while his assistant was out to lunch. The recruiter said, "I don't want to keep bothering you, but please answer one question. What's the weather in Baltimore today?"

David replied, "Rainy and cold."

"Well, in San Diego it's seventy-five and sunny. Why don't you and your wife fly out for a long weekend and check out the town and our company, all expenses paid? What do you have to lose?" It was a very effective pitch, and it led to David becoming COO of Hybritech. He did very well there. After Hybritech was acquired, he followed a similar path as that of Cam Garner and Ted Greene, launching or cofounding about a half dozen other biotech companies, including Connect, Gensia, Cancer Vax, and later his own VC firm, Hale BioPharma Ventures.

David is an effective but low-key presenter, as I saw first-hand several times. Ultimately, his demeanor didn't matter because David displayed so many other positive attributes that we've touched on in this chapter. He's quietly confident, humble, extremely competent, and hardworking. Everyone can tell that his primary motivation is helping people. He has supported his colleagues and his city as a big booster for economic development in San Diego as well as for multiple charities. All of those qualities have inspired his colleagues and investors to trust him. And that made all the difference.

RISK APPETITE: STAY HUNGRY YET CAUTIOUS

The stereotypical entrepreneur is an adrenaline junkie, placing huge bets on strategies and tactics that might make or break their startup. That might be true for a few prominent daredevils, like Elon Musk. But most successful entrepreneurs are not risk driven—they're opportunity driven. They learn how to minimize or mitigate risks, not chase them.

Of course, startups are risky by definition. But those who go out of their way to take unnecessary risks tend to fail in the long run. The more cautious and calculating risk-takers succeed. They think strategically and look for asymmetric opportunities where they might have five-to-one odds of success. Like great poker players, they have the discipline not to draw to an inside straight, even if they see others occasionally winning large pots by pursuing a high-risk strategy.

I can't recall ever meeting an entrepreneur who truly loves working on the edge and courting disaster just for the adrenaline rush. Big ideas are inherently risky, but great entrepreneurs identify an opportunity and then rigorously work to mitigate its risks. Their true competitive advantage is spotting reasonable risks, not taking crazy risks. They are generally optimistic, to be sure, but there's a big difference between optimistic and reckless. As Rob McGovern, founder of CareerBuilder, told *Fast Company*, "We make a big deal about saying 'these people are risk-takers.' It's more basic than that. It's not about being defiant. It's about the ability to calculate and mitigate."[24]

The most important way successful entrepreneurs limit risk is by figuring out whether there's a real market for their idea before wasting much capital. If possible, they put a very basic version of the product in front of customers to test demand before going wide. Their goal is to reduce the role of luck, not rely on their luck holding up.

Consultant Deborah Mills-Scofield agrees that most entrepreneurs aren't more attracted to risk than anyone else is; they just define risk differently. "For some I've known, the risk of losing autonomy and control of one's 'destiny' was far riskier than losing 'guaranteed' income and benefits. Working for someone else's company, reporting to a boss, and living under rules they weren't sure made sense were a lot riskier than creating their own business. The risk of *not* pursuing their passion, of *not* making a meaningful and significant impact on the world around them, feels much riskier than starting their own venture. . . . risk isn't as defined by losing tangibles (e.g., income, benefits, 'stuff') as it is by losing intangibles: fulfilling a passion that won't let go, defining their own sense of purpose, sating their own curiosity, looking themselves in the mirror."[25]

One great example of an inherently cautious but very successful entrepreneur is Eckard Weber, whom I've collaborated with for years at Domain. He's a master of pursuing highly ambitious startups with minimal risk by setting up opportunities for cheap and fast failure.

Eckard was born into a family of modest means in postwar Germany, which contributed to his frugality and reluctance to waste money. He worked his way through university and medical school and then came to the United States as a postdoc at Stanford to focus on medical research. When I got to know him, he was an academic at the University of California, Irvine, and could have stayed in medical research his whole career. But then he founded a startup that was acquired by one of our portfolio

THE IDEA IS THE EASY PART

companies and was invited to join the acquiring company as head of research.

My partner Jim Blair worked with him at that startup and recognized his brilliance, so we decided to bring Eckard to Domain as what we call a venture partner. Unlike a general partner, a venture partner draws a salary with the mandate to develop ideas for new startups and launch them. It was almost a hybrid role, in between entrepreneur and venture capitalist, and it gave Domain first dibs at funding his companies.

This model allowed Eckard to roll up his sleeves and launch startup after startup, almost twenty by now, based on his own ideas. This doesn't even count all the ideas he dropped before they became companies. These ideas are never aimed at modest, incremental improvements but at solving big, unmet needs, with a shot at creating massive, industry-shaking companies. This ambition may sound like a contradiction for someone I just described as risk averse. But it's not a contradiction because Eckard has refined a brilliant approach that minimizes risk without minimizing his ambitions.

He starts by observing what's going on in a given field or disease, such as obesity, Alzheimer's, and heart disease, and asking lots of questions about existing treatments. He forms a hypothesis about a possible new approach, ideally one that can find new uses for existing drugs that have already been tested and approved for safety. So much of the risk and expense of pharmaceuticals is related to safety, so avoiding those risks can give a startup a huge advantage. Eckard often looks for new uses in drugs that may first show up as a side effect. There can be tremendous value in asking whether a side effect in the treatment of X might become the desired main effect in the treatment of Y.

At any moment, Eckard might be exploring ten of these ideas, consulting his wide network of experts to develop his theories. Maybe eight of the ten will turn out to be dead ends, but Eckard can eliminate them for a relatively small cost, usually less than $100,000. Finding an experiment that quickly proves an idea is wrong is as valuable as one that keeps an idea alive. A cheap, fast failure is nearly as good as a success.

Consider his current startup, Transposon Therapeutics, Inc., which is working on a new treatment for neurodegenerative diseases, including Alzheimer's. Eckard noticed in the scientific literature that patients who have HIV and survive to old age have a greatly reduced incidence of early-onset Alzheimer's compared to that of the general population. There's some evidence suggesting a genomic connection between these seemingly unrelated conditions. Transposon's research has the potential to completely change how we fight neurodegenerative diseases.

Once he concludes that an idea might be scientifically valid, Eckard turns to a community of talented outsiders to staff a startup. Instead of putting a lot of people on a payroll, he works as much as possible with contractors—one law firm, one financial manager, one HR expert, a few contract research firms, clinical consultants, and so on. It's a plug-and-play business model, much like the movie business, where great producers and directors hire the same cinematographers and crew over and over. Then they go their separate ways when each movie is finished.

If one of Eckard's startups is making good progress with an innovative treatment, he moves on to another project, and we find an experienced, professional manager to take over. Eckard has no desire to scale something that's already working; he wants to start over with a new idea. That's how he turns the extremely risky world of pharmaceutical development into something approaching a reliable, repeatable process.

QUESTIONS TO PONDER

Before You Pursue Entrepreneurship

I won't pretend that the startup journey is equally easy for everyone, regardless of education, gender, age, temperament, skills, and so on. But at least the road is now open to everyone, and there are more good ideas out in the world than entrepreneurs to pursue them. Is your heart pulling you toward becoming one of them? Consider:

- Are you driven to create a great company that will grow, endure, serve customers, and change the world in some way? Or are you just hoping to get rich quickly?
- Are you willing to quit your day job and the stability it offers in exchange for a riskier chance at something bigger and better?
- Are you willing to work harder than you ever did in a "normal" job?

- Can you handle the pressures of being responsible for the survival of an enterprise and the fates of everyone attached to it?
- Can you balance being laser-focused on goals with being flexible on strategies and tactics to achieve those goals?
- Can you keep your wits about you in a messy situation, with no obvious path to success, and confidently direct your colleagues?
- Do you have the patience to keep plugging away, perhaps for five or ten years, before your hard work can pay off in a significant exit?

3

THE IDEA STILL COUNTS

Recognizing a "Good Enough" Opportunity and Creating a Plan

WHAT MAKES A GOOD IDEA FOR A STARTUP?

When I say that the idea is the easy part, that doesn't mean all startup ideas are basically equal. It can be a huge challenge to figure out what defines a high-potential opportunity, and it's one that comes down to two questions. First, what's a genuine unmet need—something that individuals or business customers will be so happy to have that they'll gladly pay enough to generate long-term profit for the startup? Second, why should you be the one to fill this unmet need, and will you have the capacity to do it effectively?

New entrepreneurs often go astray on either or both questions because they're in the grip of two big myths about choosing opportunities. Let's debunk those myths before we turn to a more reliable strategy for finding good startup ideas.

Myth 1: You Need a Breakthrough Invention or Exciting New Technology

A small minority of famous startups have a truly breakthrough invention that revolutionizes an entire market. These outliers, such as SpaceX and Moderna, get the lion's share of media coverage and mass attention. But most successful startups don't start with any sort of technical breakthrough. Instead, their founders often discover opportunities by seeing a tactic work in another industry, then adapting it to the industry they want to enter. Or perhaps they combine old ideas in new ways (a process I call "some assembly required," as previously mentioned).

Consider Peloton, which grew faster than anyone ever imagined before its more recent troubles. The founders started with the smart observation that it's a hassle to take spin classes, particularly in big cities. You have to reserve a slot in advance, if you can even find a session that fits your schedule. Then you have to drop whatever you're doing to get there on time. But when you get there, the trainer might be mediocre or worse. The idea of offering spin classes at home with the country's best instructors filled a genuine unmet need. It was better than a gym class and better than biking outside if you lived somewhere cold and rainy—and much better than a stationary bike in your home without an instructor to motivate you.

Another great example is Five Guys, which found a genuine unmet need within the crowded space of fast food. They saw that McDonald's and its competitors were offering fast, cheap, and average quality, but what about people who would be happy to pay more and wait longer for higher quality? That could be a potentially lucrative niche, in between traditional fast food and sit-down restaurants. So Five Guys set out to upgrade all the components they needed, sourcing better burgers, fries, buns, and so on. They proved that an idea as old as the hamburger could still provide a great opportunity for a clever startup.

One key to this kind of play is expectations management. Five Guys couldn't promise investors that they would scale like McDonald's, but they didn't need to. They just had to prove that there was a smaller but enthusiastic market. By now we know that the chain is actually in a different market from that of McDonald's, which generally ignores Five Guys. Despite McDonald's size and muscle, trying to compete with Five Guys would make McDonald's slower and more expensive, putting their primary business at risk.

Myth 2: You Can Crack an Existing Market by Building a Better Mousetrap

Most people hate change, even if a new option is objectively better than the status quo. Even B2B customers hate changes to their business processes. I've found that the biggest obstacle to progress in any field is the human instinct to say, "If it ain't broke, don't fix it."

Most demand for innovation comes from people trying to solve a problem, not make something that already exists a bit better. The same is true for most major purchases. People usually need a good reason to deviate from what they're already doing—either because they think the change will solve a problem or because they want to keep up with what their friends are buying or what the Joneses down the street are buying.

Customer loyalty to existing brands has wrecked many start-ups trying to sell a proverbial better mousetrap. Even if you can develop a better bandage to compete with Band-Aid or a better soft drink to compete with Coca-Cola, I strongly encourage you to look elsewhere. Similarly, if you're looking at a sector plagued by customer dissatisfaction, thinking you can do better, be very careful. You will need a deep understanding of exactly why that sector is fundamentally troubled, which is likely to reveal that its core problems are unsolvable. Any improvements you offer will likely only add marginal value.

A prime example is the airline industry. Virtually everyone is dissatisfied with the level of service, regardless of the carrier. But there's a fundamental reason why airlines are inherently troubled: there's almost no variable cost per passenger. It requires a huge, fixed cost to fly from point A to point B, but that cost doesn't change when you add one more passenger. So airlines will do anything to keep adding flyers, because marginal revenue from the last person to buy a ticket falls to the bottom line, and every vacant seat at takeoff is a lost opportunity. This model creates incentives to keep degrading the customer experience. *Hey, if we cut two inches from the leg room of every seat, we can fit another row in coach!* So everyone loses two inches, the snacks shrink or vanish, and everyone complains. But we keep flying because nearly every airline does the same thing. It's even hard to comparison shop on price because the airlines match each other's prices.

Improving service comes at a high cost in any field where brand loyalty is low and price sensitivity is high. Even if a new entrant could solve these structural problems, they'd just serve as a proof of concept for larger airlines to copy. There's no unfair advantage for any startup, which is why innovators like JetBlue and Virgin Atlantic have struggled. Just because an industry or market is deeply flawed doesn't make it a good opportunity.

A BETTER STRATEGY: THE FIVE CRITERIA OF GREAT STARTUP IDEAS

I judge every startup proposal by five essential issues that help me answer the two core questions: Has the startup identified a genuine unmet need, and does it have the practical ability to fill that need?

- Market: Are you addressing a true unmet need, or is it just nice to have?
- Competition: Who will be threatened by your idea, and how will they respond?

- Technology: Do you have the technical capacity to execute your idea at scale?
- Proprietary position: What's your unfair advantage that will stop others from copying your idea?
- Financial requirements: Can you generate enough cash before going broke or before your investors bail out?

If your startup idea passes these five tests, you'll be much more likely to get the capital you need. That still doesn't guarantee success, of course. Some famous startups failed these tests but still worked, while others passed all five but still flopped. It's a matter of playing the odds. Complying with all these tests may lead to a startup that's too bland, so I actually like to invest in startups that violate one or two of them if the opportunity is truly unique.

Now let's explore the five criteria with examples that show why each is so important. Quite a few of these examples are startups that failed, because I've found that you can often learn more by studying flops instead of hits.

MARKET: HOW WELL CAN YOU IDENTIFY AN UNMET NEED?

Market research has always been an inexact science, or worse. As Henry Ford famously said a century ago, "If I had asked people what they wanted, they would have said faster horses." But this doesn't mean you should avoid surveys or focus groups. Those tools are much more rigorous than they used to be, and they often yield valuable insights about a market you're considering. However, you must temper that research with intuition and common sense. Think of the market-evaluation process as both an art and a science.

Let's say you've identified what you believe to be a significant unmet need, and you've attempted to quantify the market for your solution. You could be completely wrong by either overestimating or underestimating demand. I've seen many focus groups that later declined to buy the product they were enthusiastic about when the cameras were rolling. I've also seen market researchers predict doom for products that became big hits. Even some very smart VCs thought that eBay would fail because no one would trust a stranger to ship something after they had paid for it online. Airbnb couldn't raise a penny early on, because who would let a stranger sleep on their couch or pay to sleep in a stranger's bed?

Vivus: When a Niche Becomes a Mass Market

My favorite example from personal experience is Vivus, which developed the first FDA-approved prescription drug for erectile dysfunction. As part of our market research, we surveyed internists and urologists to ask how many of their male patients were complaining of the affliction then known as impotence. Very few men were asking for help with that problem, so we assumed that the market would be small. It would be a niche drug for a relative handful of patients. Before the launch, we planned a marketing campaign to raise awareness of this rare condition. We even lobbied the NIH to change its name from impotence to ED, hoping that a new name would reduce any embarrassment that kept men away from their doctors.

But there were early signs that our analysis of the unmet need might be way off. For instance, when I visited Vivus in San Francisco for a board meeting, the driver who met me at the airport asked why I was in town. When I explained what Vivus was creating, the driver immediately asked for samples for him and his friends. Such moments led us to do focus groups, where it became clear that men with even mild or moderate symptoms were very interested. The product wasn't just for those with a serious medical problem.

Not long after, during a meeting at the FDA, the drug's reviewer asked, "How do you know this won't be used for recreational sex?" The angel on one shoulder told me to be bite my tongue, but the devil on the other shoulder forced me to reply, "What other kind is there?"

When we launched, the word of mouth was so overwhelming that Vivus was out of stock in about a week. It became the fastest-selling prescription drug ever in the first month of its launch. A few years later, we lost that record to Pfizer, with its launch of Viagra.

Cilco: Reframing the Incentives for Customers

Rorer acquired a startup, Cilco, that developed the first artificial intraocular lens to treat cataracts. Millions of older people suffer from cataracts as the lens inside one or both eyes gets cloudy. Eyesight comes from both the lens and the cornea, and the treatment for severe cataracts, for decades, was surgical removal of the lens. Patients could still see with their corneas alone, but they couldn't focus on anything without extremely thick and unattractive glasses that looked like the bottoms of old-fashioned Coke bottles.

Cilco's innovation enabled surgeons to remove cloudy lenses from the eyes and replace them with artificial lenses that were just as good as or even better than the originals. The patient's eyesight would return to 20/20, without needing any glasses at all, let alone Coke-bottle ones. It was an amazing medical breakthrough.

As we prepared to market these intraocular lenses, we studied the statistics about cataract surgery. It was an uncommon procedure. Most older people diagnosed with cataracts simply tolerated their cloudy vision. Many would die or become mentally incapacitated before their cataracts got bad enough to cause blindness.

But when we launched the intraocular lens, ophthalmologists were deluged with patients requesting the new surgery, far beyond our projections. Now that the result would be life without needing any glasses at all, the cost–benefit equation was completely different. Before long, the number of patients getting cataract surgery was up dramatically compared to the era before the intraocular lens. The new technology had essentially transformed the perception of how bad the disease was. It was a surprise happy ending in this case, but not all failures of market research and mathematical projections end so happily.

Novalar: The Illusion of an Unmet Need

Novalar, a startup funded by Domain, invented a dental drug that would get rid of the numbness caused by lidocaine during dental procedures. After a cavity filling or root canal, this new drug could make your face feel normal in minutes, instead of staying numb for another two or three hours. A survey of dentists asked if they wanted it for their patients, and they overwhelmingly did. So Novalar went through the lengthy and expensive process of development, testing, approvals, production, and marketing.

But the market research turned out to be disconnected from reality. It gave the illusion of an unmet need where one didn't really exist. Dentists said they wanted the drug, but they had little to no interest in selling it to their patients as an add-on service. Doctors and dentists generally hate to sell anything—they see selling as beneath the dignity of their profession. This was especially true in this case because the drug wouldn't be covered by insurance, since its purpose was comfort rather than necessity.

We urged dentists to add the drug to the standard treatment process, raising the price of the overall treatment to cover it. They could have announced it as a wonderful new service, not an option that patients could take or leave. But most chose not to go that way. Expecting dentists to sell an option that patients considered unnecessary was doomed, and asking them to absorb the cost was similarly doomed.

With no enthusiasm from dentists, and no word of mouth driving patient demand, the startup failed.

Orexigen: Making Fatal Assumptions About Your Market

Domain invested in Orexigen Therapeutics to tackle obesity, a huge problem in the United States that increases the risks of many serious medical conditions, including heart disease and diabetes. After meeting with a panel of obesity experts, my partner Eckard Weber came up with a great idea, a perfect example of "some assembly required."* We could combine two preexisting drugs: an antidepressant and an anti-addiction drug that had the side effect of suppressing appetite. Since both had already been tested for safety and effectiveness, it was highly likely that our combination drug, Contrave, would win approval as a new way to fight obesity.

Orexigen recruited a first-class team, and preliminary clinical trials showed that patients taking Contrave lost more weight than did those in a placebo group.† We made an alliance with a bigger pharmaceutical company to promote the drug to doctors. Unfortunately, it never successfully penetrated the obesity market, even after we reacquired the rights and raised substantial financing to take a shot at marketing directly to consumers. Ultimately, the company went into bankruptcy and had to be sold off as a loss.

Our big mistake was assuming that we already understood the market instead of applying better market research and

---

* We met Eckard in chapter two as someone who loves launching companies rather than running them indefinitely.

† The difference was statistically significant for modest weight loss but not for dramatic weight loss.

common sense. We knew that obesity was a serious medical problem that raised the risk of premature death for millions. But we failed to recognize that during a typical fifteen-minute visit, most primary care doctors focus on whatever immediate problem is affecting an obese patient rather than start a conversation regarding weight loss.

We also failed to realize that despite the health risks of obesity, most people seek weight-loss treatment because they want to look better. Contrave was more appealing to someone who wanted to lose five or ten pounds, particularly since weight loss after taking the drug was modest, rather than to extremely obese patients. Yet our marketing had targeted the latter group.

It's easy to get excited about a product that feels like the next surefire hit. But you have to dig into the practical details of your target market, not just its theoretical potential size.

COMPETITION: WHAT'S YOUR EDGE, AND WHOSE LUNCH ARE YOU TRYING TO EAT?

Studying the competition requires a clear-eyed look at who you'll be up against if you enter a sector and whether you have a real, defensible advantage. Have your potential competitors already tried to offer something similar? Might they have anything new in the pipeline? Do you think you have more expertise than they do? Perhaps the most important question: Who will be hurt if your startup succeeds, and how far will those competitors go to protect the status quo? What can they do to thwart you?

Any large company has advantages against a startup because of its existing infrastructure, customer relationships, supplier relationships, and easy access to additional capital. So if you're trying to improve an existing product or service, you will be at a huge disadvantage relative to the big guys.

Some founders think they can minimize this disadvantage by only going after a small slice of an existing market. This is an old myth that goes back at least to the 1970s, when tech startups used to say, "If we can just get one percent of IBM's market share, we can make a fortune. They're so big that they won't even notice." That strategy didn't work back then, and it still doesn't. Large incumbents will fight you for every scrap of market share because their executives are rewarded or punished based on small shifts in market share. They have the staff and resources to constantly scan the horizon for new threats, which makes flying under the radar almost impossible.

Once they spot you, they will fight you by any means necessary, fair or otherwise. Let's look at some ways that those fights can play out.

Align, Revisited: When Partners See You as a Threat

As we saw in chapter one, orthodontists weren't excited at first about Align's amazing innovation. Many feared that Invisalign might threaten their monopoly on straightening teeth. Orthodontists could see that since Invisalign was easier to implement, dentists could become their competition instead of their source of referrals.

Align overcame this reluctance thanks to a rapid and enthusiastic response by consumers, which is rare in any field. All the company had to do was show adults considering orthodonture what Invisalign could do and urge them to ask a dentist or orthodontist about it. If these patients went to an orthodontist who tried to steer them toward traditional braces, they simply left to find a different provider. Under pressure from their own patients, nearly all orthodontists soon adopted Invisalign. And they ultimately benefited because their adult practice boomed.

Align was an interesting contrast to the development of arthroscopic surgery in the 1980s. Early on, we knew that arthroscopy was a better way to do many kinds of surgical procedures, much easier on the patient because the incisions were so small. But orthopedic surgeons resisted new practices that went counter to their training and expertise. Unlike orthodontists, surgeons had to learn a whole new way to handle their daily procedures. For instance, instead of cutting open a knee and looking directly inside, they had to view it through a tiny scope and manipulate instruments like in a computer game. We were rarely able to convince established orthopedic surgeons to learn the new procedures. Instead, we had to focus on the next generation of surgeons in the early phase of their careers, who had no loyalty to traditional procedures.

Reva: When One Innovation Loses to Another

A cardiac stent is a tiny, straw-like tube that surgeons implant into the heart of a patient to keep blood flowing smoothly through the coronary arteries. But blood had a tendency to clot inside stents after about a year, creating a blockage that could lead to another heart attack. Or else it might require a second round of surgery to replace the stent. Either way, "in-stent restenosis" was a serious problem.

In 2000, a startup called Reva invented a new kind of stent that would be absorbed into the body after a year. This was a great idea because it would eliminate the problem of clogging. What we didn't consider when evaluating it was that a bigger company might be developing other solutions to the stent problem. Sure enough, Boston Scientific was working on a new lubricant that would coat the inside of a traditional stent with drugs that prevented clotting. It would be almost like WD-40 or motor oil for the heart. By the time our new stent was ready to launch, the problem it was designed to solve had already been solved.

We had looked at the competition, but we hadn't properly looked at potential future competition. Surgeons would much rather add a better lubricant to coat the inside of the stents they were used to inserting than try something new. Reva had to pivot to another challenge (leg clots), but Domain sold off its stake to cut any further losses.

MicroSurge: When the Competition Hits Back Hard

MicroSurge was a startup that made non-disposable medical instruments. Its innovation was that while most medical instruments had to be discarded or recycled after a single use, this new kind of instrument would have just a small disposable piece, with the rest reusable. This approach would reduce waste and save money for hospitals and medical practices. The startup planned to undercut the competition on pricing.

The problem was that we failed to understand how hard our competition—the big medical-device producers—would fight to squash this alternative. As noted earlier, you can't fly under the radar of a Fortune 500 company. From their perspective, you're not merely trying to eat their lunch; you're trying to burn down their kitchen. So they will do anything possible to crush you.

Some founders also assume that if the big guys feel threatened by an innovation, they can simply license it from the innovator. In this case, the big companies could have enjoyed the benefits of lower production costs and reduced waste. But giants like Johnson & Johnson already had an extensive product line and a huge installed base of customers who would need to change their established buying patterns for surgical instruments. Those companies were selling millions of disposable products every year. Even if their customers were willing to switch, it would be a major effort and expense to change all that production capacity. From the perspective of the big companies, it wasn't worth it to license MircoSurge designs, no matter how good they were or how much they might reduce costs in the long run.

The startup also made a third faulty assumption: underestimating the power of offering a full line of products at a discount, aka "bundling." J&J and others offered hospitals deep discounts if they signed up for a package deal of many kinds of instruments, sutures, drapes, gowns, and other products. They had the margin to make hospitals an offer on bundles that they couldn't refuse. MicroSurge's sales reps had no chance to crack the markets for any of its reusable products.

It was a classic failure to analyze who was going to be hurt by this new approach and anticipate how the competition might defend itself. Some smarter analysis might have kept MicroSurge from launching its non-disposable instruments business. Instead, the startup essentially went out of business, getting sold for small money at a big loss.

TECHNOLOGY: CAN YOU REALLY BUILD IT?

It's tempting to think that cool new technology is enough to make a startup work, but technology won't matter if the other criteria don't line up. I have several key questions for any tech-driven startup: Will the technology work as promised? If so, can it be done at a reasonable cost? How much time and effort will be required to make it work? How many things have to go right for it to be successful?

You can get in big trouble if you start with a high-tech solution and then look for a question it can answer. For instance, the Segway electric scooter was a very impressive technology because its automatic balancing mechanism made it easy to ride with minimal skill or practice. But after launching with a ton of media attention and word of mouth, it never found a "killer app" usage to generate demand beyond the initial wave of curiosity. Its developers searched in vain for an unmet need the Segway could fill, so it remained merely a "nice to have" product for people who bought expensive toys.

Conversely, you can also get in trouble by overpromising on technology that can't quite do in practice what seems possible in theory. I was reminded of this while following the downfall of Theranos and its now infamous CEO, Elizabeth Holmes. Her ambitious goal—a small machine that could analyze a very small blood sample in a drugstore or doctor's office, eliminating the need to send large blood samples to a lab—would have filled a genuinely unmet need. The potential was sky-high, but making it work would require solving six or seven separate technical challenges. It appears that Holmes underestimated the multiplier effect that governs such situations—a law of math that I learned at a very steep cost (see below).

TransCell: The Multiplier Effect of Technical Challenges

Suppose you have to solve five problems to make a device work, and the theoretical odds of each being solved is 90 percent. What are the odds of the overall project succeeding? Many assume that the answer is also 90 percent. But it's actually 0.9 * 0.9 * 0.9 * 0.9 * 0.9, which equals 59 percent. If the average success rate of each challenge drops to 85 percent, the overall success rate drops to just 44 percent. Sadly, instead of learning this in Statistics 101 in college (where I was a math major!) or in business school, I lost a lot of Domain's money to finally get it.

TransCell was a startup working on an artificial pancreas, which in theory could radically improve the lives of people living with diabetes by replacing their own faulty pancreas and eliminating their frequent need for blood-sugar testing and insulin injections. In the early 1990s, the founders of TransCell had a genuinely big idea: take pancreas cells from pigs, whose pancreas is very close to humans', and put them in a bag inside the patient. In theory, a porous bag could detect the level of glucose in the blood, which is how the pancreas works, and then it could release insulin to balance the glucose at an optimal level.

This was a great idea, but it required solving five separate technical problems. First, TransCell had to find a way to harvest pancreatic cells from a compatible pig and keep them viable until they could be implanted. Second, it had to create a mesh bag to hold the pancreatic cells, using a biocompatible substance that the patient's immune system wouldn't reject. Third, the bag needed to be strong enough to block the patient's white blood cells from getting inside and attacking the pig's pancreatic cells. Fourth, the bag had to be porous enough that the pancreatic cells could detect the level of glucose in the bloodstream, which would trigger the production of insulin only when the body needed it. Finally, the bag needed holes big enough to release the insulin into the bloodstream, but not so big that they would allow an attack on the pancreatic cells.

Most of those problems had already been solved by bioengineers, but never at the same time for the same medical device. For the TransCell team, it was like trying to solve a Rubik's

Cube—fixing each problem created one or more additional problems. The holes in the mesh were always too big or too small, never exactly right. Iterating over and over cost a lot of time and money until we all had to admit that the effort was doomed, no matter how long we kept tinkering.

When a new product doesn't require any breakthrough science or technology, non-tech people will sometimes dismissively say, "It's just engineering." Those words scare the hell out of me, because engineering is hard! As an outsider, it's easy to assume that folks in tech can tweak this or that until it works perfectly. But sometimes it's just not possible to solve multiple challenges at the same time.

This is another situation where the mythology of inventors and entrepreneurs distorts our perceptions of reality. We've all heard the story of Thomas Edison iterating a thousand different versions of his first light bulb until he finally found a combination of components that worked well. That approach might work if you're a lone genius in a private lab, but not if you're running a startup that needs to stay under budget and hit the revenue targets set by investors.

Athena Neurosciences: Sometimes Partial Progress Is All You Need

More than $100 billion is spent annually on treatment for Alzheimer's disease, which afflicts an estimated 6.5 million Americans in the most heartbreaking ways. Almost all of that spending is palliative because there is no known way to prevent or treat the disease. After decades of research failures, most of the Big Pharma companies have given up on Alzheimer's research to focus on more promising challenges.

In the late 1980s, Domain invested in Athena Neurosciences, which was working on a bold new approach to fighting Alzheimer's. One frustration for researchers was that they couldn't diagnose the disease in mice or other mammals because there was no way to do cognitive testing. Some scientists even believed that Alzheimer's was exclusive to humans. Athena's big idea was to isolate the human genes that generate plaque in the brain, a symptom of Alzheimer's, and implant them in mice. Once they could confirm that the mice had the disease, it would open up a world of new research opportunities. Potential therapies could be tried that would never be allowed in human trials, especially with patients who were no longer able to give informed consent.

Before Athena could even start to apply this new testing ability to drugs that might slow or reverse Alzheimer's, it was acquired by Elan for $625 million. The startup didn't need to get all the way to curing the disease to be recognized for a massive technological innovation. Athena showed that you don't necessarily need to solve every aspect of a huge problem to create a valuable startup. Sometimes the opportunity lies in one particularly thorny aspect of the overall problem.

PROPRIETARY POSITION: CAN YOU DEFEND YOUR INTELLECTUAL PROPERTY?

This consideration follows naturally from the technology question. If you do succeed in solving your technical challenges, can you protect the intellectual property of the innovation that powers your startup? Can you acquire patents? If so, the government will give you a seventeen-year exclusive on your idea, which might be a critical competitive advantage. Conversely, is your new product or process going to infringe on anyone else's patents? Domain invests considerable time and effort with patent attorneys to avert potential IP disasters.

Unfortunately, patent law is part of civil law, not criminal, which means the government won't step in and police violations. It's your responsibility as a patent holder to sue anyone infringing on your patent. But that kind of lawsuit can be extremely time consuming and expensive, which can derail an otherwise promising startup.

Big companies can be very hypocritical about intellectual property—talking about how essential it is to protect it, then turning around and stealing it from a startup to defend their existing position. This is yet another risk you need to be mindful of. If you're going to build any kind of business around intellectual property, you have to be sure your IP is defensible in practice, not just in theory.

If you recall my evaluation of Align Technology in chapter one, one of the most impressive things about that startup was its smart IP strategy. The founders applied for a patent for using three or more aligners to straighten teeth, in contrast to the way traditional braces work. This patent wasn't tied to the specific material being used in the aligners, which gave them a wide range of tactical options and blocked off competition from other potential producers of aligners. The technology for the original Invisalign was difficult to refine, but they had a proprietary position that gave them enough time to work out the bugs before anyone could copy them.

Cardiac Science: When You Can't Enforce Your Own Patent

In contrast to Align's skillful use of patents, Cardiac Science found itself stymied and ultimately wrecked by an unenforceable patent. The startup developed a more advanced defibrillator for people suffering a heart attack, one that included an automatic analyzer to tell nonmedical professionals exactly when to activate the device, based on the patient's vital signs. This was a technological breakthrough, and Cardiac Science was able to win a patent for it.

But then a big competitor took the same idea and developed a similar version of the same product. Once they had their own version of a defibrillator that could tell the user when to activate it, this competitor used their existing market penetration and deep pockets to commercialize it. In other words, to our surprise, the big firm brazenly ignored Cardiac Science's patent.

We had grounds to sue for patent infringement, and we did. But it soon became clear that our competitor would make this an extremely expensive and time-consuming lawsuit, with no guarantee we would prevail in court. They had all the time in the world to drag it out with endless depositions, motions, and requests for discovery. We were looking at several years of litigation, with an estimated cost of $15 million per year to deploy a team of expert IP lawyers.

The other side was clearly willing to spend tens of millions in legal fees to defend billions in potential future revenues. But Cardiac Science didn't have the resources to make and sell defibrillators while simultaneously waging a legal war against a major competitor. The risk–reward calculation just didn't make sense, so Cardiac Science had to walk away from the product.

Sometimes, having intellectual property on your side isn't enough. It comes back to whose lunch is going to get eaten, how threatened they will feel, and how far they will go to defend their market share. These questions often seem to be more about psychology than about business or law. Like a chess player or poker player, you've got to think a few moves ahead and anticipate what the other side will or won't do. To be safe, assume the worst about their respect for fair play, or lack thereof.

FINANCIAL REQUIREMENTS: CAN YOU STAY SOLVENT UNTIL YOU REACH PROFITABILITY?

This final criterion requires evaluating how much capital you will need to raise to reach key milestones on the road to viability and sustainability. The less money it will take to make clear progress, the more appealing your startup will be to early-stage investors. They will want proof of concept as quickly and cheaply as possible, as you'll see in the next chapter on how VCs think. Once you have proof of concept, it will be much easier to raise additional rounds of financing.

For instance, suppose you have a drug that promises to be better than current drugs at lowering blood pressure. You'd have to test it against existing medicines as well as against a placebo and against doing nothing. Those double-blind trials can cost $100 million or more, before you even find out if you have a shot at a viable business. There are no intermediate milestones; it either works or it doesn't. I've learned the hard way to avoid those kinds of startups because it's too expensive to potentially find yourself on a dead-end street.

Instead, I look for startups that might require lots of capital to scale up in the long run but have clear intermediate benchmarks that won't cost a fortune to evaluate in the short run and medium run. The classic example is a new food product, like a breakfast cereal, that can be test-marketed in a few corners of the country before an expensive national rollout. Try to find an opportunity where you can make it around the bases one at a time instead of one whose only alternatives are hitting a home run or striking out.

I can imagine being a VC in 1971, listening to Fred Smith pitch his idea to launch Federal Express. Fred might have said, "My vision is a private, national delivery system that's faster and better than the US Postal Service. I'll charge people a premium for overnight delivery. Here's my market research confirming that

98 percent of those surveyed would love to have overnight delivery guaranteed."

I would have politely asked Fred to leave immediately. The fixed costs to launch FedEx would have been staggering, with all those planes, trucks, transit hubs, and other infrastructure, not to mention hiring a huge nationwide staff. And his research about customer demand wouldn't have impressed me. Of course people *say* they want fast delivery, but how many would actually pay for it at the moment of choice?

As with a blood-pressure drug, the only way to find out if FedEx was truly viable was to spend hundreds of millions and hope for the best. There were no real intermediate benchmarks before investors could see if it would work or not. FedEx did work, of course, revolutionizing the shipping business and giving early investors a huge payoff. But it was an extreme outlier. Its success doesn't change the fact that the original idea wasn't investor-friendly, with a series of benchmarks over a number of rounds. It was another example of a poker player drawing to an inside straight and making luck appear to be genius.

Instead of chasing long shots, choose a startup with milestones that will quickly prove or disprove viability for a relatively small investment. Then you can course-correct if you hit a disappointing milestone, or else cut your losses and abandon the idea. Either option is far better than taking something all the way from invention through development, production, and marketing before finally discovering a fatal flaw.

Big Capital Equipment: When It Takes Too Long to Generate Revenue

Being mindful of financial requirements isn't just about considering how much you'll need to spend to establish your business; it's also about how long it will take to start generating significant revenue. Many founders underestimate the bumps in the road that can delay positive cash flow from operations. That's why Domain rarely invests in companies that want to innovate in medical diagnostic equipment, such as MRIs and CT scan machines. Those are major investments for hospitals, which treat them as a capital improvement rather than a routine purchase. The resulting sales cycle can easily stretch out for a year or more.

One startup that we declined to fund tried to persuade hospital oncology departments to invest millions in a new diagnostic machine that would elevate their success rates with cancer patients. After getting the doctors on board, it needed to convince hospital engineering departments that the machine would be logistically feasible to set up and maintain in an insulated room. Then it had to sell each hospital's CFO, who would demand a cost–benefit analysis. Finally, the hospital president and possibly also the board had to approve. They might try to raise money from a donor to sponsor the new machine, with naming rights, which could add many more months to the sales cycle.

In venture capital, the old saying is true: time is money. We watched this startup launch with far too little capital in reserve, leading to its collapse before it could get to sustainable positive cash flow.

QUESTIONS TO PONDER
On Choosing Opportunities

- Are you truly addressing an unmet need, or are you offering something that your potential customers could easily live without?
- What incentive will they have to switch from whatever they're using now to whatever you're offering?
- Can you overcome their innate resistance to change?
- How reliable is your research into the competition—not just existing players but anyone else who might enter your space before you get off the ground?
- If your idea is so good, why hasn't anyone thought of it sooner? Or do you really think you can simply execute it better than anyone else?
- How hard will it be to make the technology work?
- Once you start operating, how hard will it be to prevent others from copying you?
- Does your financial model make sense? Will you start making money before you run out of capital?
- Are there good intermediate benchmarks to prove that you're on the right path before you burn too much capital?

For these and other questions, you will be tempted to give optimistic answers and assume everything will go the way you hope. But please remember that the cost of discarding a startup idea before you launch is zero. In fact, each idea you discard will make you a little better at evaluating the next idea that crosses your mind.

4

WHAT VCs LOOK FOR
The Care and Feeding of Your Investors

SHARK TANK IS FICTION

Getting funding might be the entrepreneurship subject accompanied with the most, and the most damaging, misinformation. This chapter debunks the myths that people absorb from all those entertaining but misleading pitch-meeting scenes in movies and TV shows.

For instance, *Shark Tank* makes people think that getting financing is all about describing your startup in just a couple of minutes, thereby charming investors who will evaluate your pitch on the spot and make an immediate offer. Then the startup founder might negotiate, perhaps asking for $10 million instead of a shark's offer of $5 million. They go back and forth for a minute, then land on $7 million. That made-for-TV scenario couldn't be further from what really happens.

VCs actually make funding decisions based on a complex web of factors. Some are quantifiable metrics about market demand, competition, potential growth, proprietary position, and so on. Others are less tangible impressions of a startup's management team, narrative, internal chemistry, and feel for the customer. Not everything important can be easily measured. Good VCs draw on both sides of their brains, studying every fact and figure they can get their hands on while also honing their gut instincts. They see investing as both a science and an art.

This chapter will give you some general guidelines and warnings about pitching investors for startup capital. As always, I'm not trying to compile a complete step-by-step guide to the entire process. If you're wondering what font looks best on a PowerPoint slide, you can find good tutorials on YouTube. My goal, rather, is to stick to the big picture: what will increase or decrease your odds of getting the capital you need to grow and thrive.

Please note that VCs are not monolithic. We each approach things differently, and some will disagree with various points I'm about to make. But in general, the many VCs I've known have the same basic red flags and green flags, and understanding their perspective is invaluable so their actions will make more sense to you. For instance, you want additional funds so you can make your great idea better, but a VC wants to know how much it will cost to prove that your idea is actually bad. You want as much money as you can get, all at once, but a VC wants to invest in a series of rounds. Knowing how they see things will help you get to the best possible outcome.

VENTURE CAPITAL IS A PARTNERSHIP, NOT A TRANSACTION

Perhaps the most important thing to remember is that seeking venture capital is the first step in building a partnership, not merely doing a transaction. It's not like buying or selling a used car, where it's all about getting good value for a product that can be evaluated with reasonable objectivity based on mileage, engine condition, body damage, and so on.

In a partnership, unlike a transaction, neither party has an incentive to squeeze every possible dollar out of the other, because you have to collaborate long after you sign a deal. A VC will usually join a startup's board of directors, which is a legal commitment to maximize the value of the company. Also, a VC can't easily unwind their investment. After you buy a publicly traded stock, you can sell it whenever you want, but a VC who buys a piece of your startup is stuck with it until the company is sold or goes public. And if it fails, that's not just a financial loss; it's a hit to the VC's reputation. (When I eventually do my last deal and stop caring about my reputation, watch out!)

Instead of lowballing you, a good VC would much rather do an accurate valuation and make a fair offer so they can start off the partnership on the right foot. It's not about being nice or generous; it's about maximizing their own long-term profits. After all, if the startup hits its milestone goals and takes off, you will both win.

Understanding these incentives will hopefully reduce your anxiety about the process of pitching for capital. Like a car salesman, a VC is constantly doing these deals, while you might do just one every five years or more. So in both situations, an outsider faces a huge disadvantage in experience and knowledge.

YOUR BIGGEST POTENTIAL MISTAKE: EXAGGERATING (OR OUTRIGHT LYING)

Before you do anything else in this process, you need to put some boundaries on your expectations. Even if you've chosen a solid business idea—based on the criteria in the previous chapter—you have no idea how successful your startup might actually become. The range of potential problems and obstacles is infinite, and they can interact in infinite combinations. So try to stick to the facts and avoid grandiose terms like "revolutionary" or "breakthrough" or "paradigm-shifting." You can think of this process as exploring the potential value of your startup, not demanding whatever it might be worth in the best of all possible outcomes.

You might encounter advice to put conservative, realistic, and worst-case forecasts in your pitch. You can try that as a useful exercise, but any decent VC knows that financial forecasts are essentially fiction. None of my most successful companies have ever come close to hitting the worst-case projections in their proposals—they weren't that good! And their more optimistic projections were always a distant fantasy. That's why I almost always ignore the numbers themselves in a business plan, whether they're labeled as best-case, probable-case, or worst-case scenarios. The premises and assumptions you're making will be more revealing than the numbers you present.

Founders who exaggerate risk blow their best shot at capital, even if many other factors are running in their favor. When I meet with an entrepreneur, I generally ask what they think their pre-money valuation* should be. But I don't use their answer to calculate an offer; I use it to gauge their state of mind, especially whether they have delusions of grandeur. If the founder replies something like, "This is the biggest thing ever, it's worth $100 million right now," I will probably pass on that deal. There are too many other potential deals to get stuck in a partnership with a chronic exaggerator.

For instance, I once met with a doctor who invented an automatic defibrillator that people could keep in their home and pull off the shelf when someone was having a heart attack. His pitch projected that every family in the country would want to buy one. When I asked how he planned to market his product to that

---

* Defined as the value of the company excluding any additional capital infusion.

huge customer base, he replied, "I'm not worried about marketing because the appeal is so obvious. It will sell itself. The only thing I'm worried about is whether we can find enough trucks to distribute all those millions of units." The process of getting funding may seem daunting, but if you can avoid delusions of grandeur, you'll already be way ahead of that doctor.

At every stage, try to be open and forthright about your start-up's weaknesses along with its strengths. As you'll see ahead, during due diligence, any good VC will check what you say with the appropriate experts, so you can save everyone time by being a straight shooter.

WHEN TO SEEK FUNDING

Shark Tank and similar media make it seem like your best strategy is getting outside capital as soon as you can. The rationale seems to be that you should spend as little of your own money as possible to get your startup off the ground. Actually, the smarter strategy is the opposite: seek funding as late as possible.

Long before you pitch outside investors, try to get off the ground via your own savings, personal loans from friends and family, credit cards, a home equity loan, or any other sources you can think of. Venture funding is not only difficult to get but also very expensive because you have to give up a portion of your ownership. VCs equate the value of a startup with the risk that it will fail. The further you travel along the road to success before raising money, the less risky your startup will seem and the more likely that VCs will want to invest. Conversely, the earlier you pitch, the bigger the chunk you will have to give away, which can seriously hurt your long-term payoff.

If you can finance the first $100,000 yourself (or via friends and family) before seeking investors, that's great. If you and two cofounders can put in $100,000 each, that's better. Of course, $500,000 would be even better. But it's not just about the absolute numbers. It's about proving the founding team's commitment to the venture. If you can show angel investors or VCs that you have serious skin in the game, they will take you more seriously and value your startup more favorably. The last thing you want to signal is that you don't feel bullish enough to risk a lot of your personal resources.

Here are some key questions to help you decide when it's a good time to start pitching for venture financing:

- If you're building a product, do you have a working prototype yet? Pitching investors is far easier if you can do show-and-tell.
- If you need patents to make your business defensible, have you obtained them yet? Or have you at least applied for patents via a reputable patent attorney?
- Have you figured out your management lineup, especially for key roles such as CEO, CFO, CTO, and VP of sales? Are the people in those roles qualified and experienced?

- If you're a scientist or techie with no business background, are you sure you have the skills to be CEO? Will you consider giving that role to an experienced manager?
- How much market research have you done, even amateur or non-quantitative research? No VC will believe in your market potential just on your gut instinct.

GOING FOR IT

If your answers to these questions convince you that you're ready to seek outside investors, it's important to work through the following distinct steps.

Step One: Researching Who to Pitch

Common sense might suggest that the more VCs you reach out to, the more likely you are to get one of them to say yes. But that's not how this industry works. Less can be more, and more can be extremely off-putting. Whenever I receive a business plan labeled something like "Copy #976, highly confidential," I reach for my delete button. Don't insult VCs by signaling that you're desperately trying every possible source of funding. You have to show that you've done your homework and picked a small pool of potential investors who might be a good fit for your kind of startup.

Be thorough in researching the VCs who funded other companies in your space or who might have a natural affinity for your product. Remember Peloton from the previous chapter? Venture capitalists in California didn't get the concept because their culture was all about biking outside in the sunshine. It wasn't until the founders pitched some VCs in New York City that anyone saw the potential.

Once you find some relevant investors, look for networking connections to them. Try to find a friend of a friend to refer you so you're not just a stranger knocking on the door. A good mutual connection might be a lawyer, banker, or executive at a company the VC has already funded. It can also be anyone credible in the VC's network who knows you and can say nice things about you. LinkedIn is a great resource to find common connections and craft a small number of personal emails rather than blast out a mass mailing. Try the five best connections you can find, then continue to add more if necessary. It might take a while to do this kind of networking, but sooner or later there's usually a way to get to any investor via a warm introduction.

In the meantime, resist the temptation to blast out an impersonalized pitch; it almost certainly won't work. Most VCs delete cold pitches without even replying. Domain sends a polite reply, at least, but after nearly thirty-five years, I don't think we've ever funded a single proposal that came in over the transom. I assume some VCs must still be open to unrequested pitches from strangers; otherwise, we wouldn't be getting so many of them. But I don't know any reputable VC firms that do deals with total strangers.

Step Two: Writing a Brief Summary Email

Business plans are highly overrated. Every startup guru talks about them, and every entrepreneurship class makes them seem like the key to impressing investors. You can drive yourself crazy trying to write a fifty- or seventy-five-page document filled with buzzwords and jargon that make you sound sophisticated.

In reality, you don't need anywhere near that degree of detail, at least not yet, and you definitely don't need fancy business jargon. The large majority of deals we end up doing start with a brief summary email, about 500 to 750 words. The goal at that point is to convince a VC to grant you a meeting, not to actually agree to an investment. In the simplest, clearest language possible, summarize your idea, why your target audience will pay for it, and why your startup team has an unfair advantage to deliver it. Then stop and ask for a meeting to go into more detail. If you send a VC an exhaustive business plan at this early stage, you will (1) exhaust their patience, and (2) risk giving them reasons, hidden somewhere in the details, to reject you.

At this early point, VCs don't need the details of how a new technology works or the methods and protocols that prove its effectiveness. All of that can wait for the pitch meeting or the due-diligence stage. For now, we just want to know that you seem competent as a founder, that you are coming to us from a trusted mutual contact, and that you can frame a simple narrative: *what* the startup is doing, *why* consumers will care, and *how* it will make money. Tell us *briefly* about the unmet need you've identified and your proprietary idea for filling that need.

If you can do that in your email, you might be invited to come in for a pitch meeting. Then the real fun begins.

Step Three: Writing a Pitch Deck and Supporting Proposal

If you get invited to spend an hour at a VC firm, that doesn't mean you should create an hour-long PowerPoint presentation. Aim for a deck that will only take thirty minutes to present, which will leave plenty of time for questions and conversation. Most of the technical and financial details can go into a leave-behind proposal that the VCs can scrutinize after you leave—assuming they're still interested after hearing your presentation.

One good way to structure your deck and handout is to work through the five major criteria of a good startup idea, which we covered in chapter three:

- **Market:** What is the unmet need? Why will anybody want this? Will potential customers be willing to switch from whatever they're using now? How big is the potential market?
- **Competition:** Who else is trying to meet this need? Why haven't they done it already? What can competitors do to block you by meeting the same need sooner, better, more cheaply, or at a bigger scale?

- **Technology:** Do you have the technical capacity to fill this need? Are you qualified to execute on your plan?
- **Proprietary position:** Once you start filling this need, how will you make sure others won't copy the business and fill it the same way? What patents do you need to protect your IP? How far along are you toward getting them?
- **Financial requirements:** How long will you have to spend investment capital before the startup can become financially self-sustainable?

On top of those criteria, make sure your deck and proposal explain the backgrounds of your management team. What have you done before, in the startup world or elsewhere? What obstacles have you overcome? It's not about flashy credentials; it's about proving a record of accomplishment and skills.

Try to highlight comparable startups that have received funding in your field. VCs will look at deals that are similar to yours in the same sector or a closely related one. You will gain a big advantage if you research successful recent startups that can be plausible comps. It signals to VCs that you're thinking the same way they do.

It's also important to include realistic goals, milestones, and timelines. What is your startup really trying to accomplish? You want to find a happy medium between "not ambitious enough" and "wildly unrealistic." The timeline is your road map, flagging intermediate milestones that will help you stay on track. VCs love milestones that are easy to track. The last thing we want is to sink millions into a startup whose progress is a total mystery until very far along in the progress, with no short-term visibility into how it's going or opportunity for course correction. I call that a "yup/nope" startup because it can cost a fortune to finally reach a binary outcome—it either works or it doesn't, with little room for modification along the way. I almost always pass on yup/nope startups because the second-best thing to succeeding is failing fast and cheap!

For instance, let's say you're starting a company to develop a new cancer drug. Your proposal should include the stages of development and testing, with a rough timeline for each. Research how long those stages took for similar startups. Don't exaggerate, because VCs will spot any wildly optimistic estimates. And remember that everything always takes longer than you think it will. You might get lucky and find smooth sailing at every stage, but never *promise* to get lucky.

Finally, tie your milestones explicitly to the capital you're looking for. Try to keep the request simple. If a VC gives you $X, you will spend 30 percent of it on A, B, and C in the first quarter, followed by 25 percent of it on D and E in the second quarter, and so on. If possible, also flag what additional capital you may be looking for down the road after early milestones have been met. But avoid getting into the weeds of how much equity you're willing to give up—that's a question for later.

Step Four: Telling a Compelling Story at the Pitch Meeting

Let's say it's the big day, and you're about to set up in a VC's conference room. You have your handouts printed, and you've rehearsed your thirty-minute presentation enough times to get comfortable with it. Take a deep breath—there's no need to panic about your presentation skills. We don't expect you to be as charming as George Clooney or as compelling in a boardroom as Steve Jobs.

We do, however, expect you to be deeply knowledgeable about your startup, its market, and the challenges it will face. We expect you to speak clearly and articulately. If you can't, you might need outside coaching in advance, along with your rehearsals. I also strongly recommend role-playing for the Q&A part of the meeting so that you can anticipate all the tough questions and practice your answers.

Keep in mind that thirty minutes is *not* an elevator pitch—it should be plenty of time to make a clear and compelling case, as long as you avoid overloading your deck with too much data or technical details. We don't need to know all the bells and whistles of your technology in this meeting. You can put that information into your handout, and we will ask plenty of questions during the due-diligence phase. Instead of wasting time to explain how the product works, show us who will care if it does work.

Remember, we're not only evaluating the opportunity—we are simultaneously evaluating *you* as the founder. What did you think is most important to convey in this room? Do you come across as most obsessed with the technology, the numbers, or the opportunity to serve your customers? Or, worst of all, with stroking your own ego?

It can be hard to simplify a complicated technology, but you have to give it your best shot. Domain once financed a startup working on antisense gene therapy, a technology that could be applied to eight or nine different diseases but was hard to explain quickly and simply. As a result, we struggled to pitch it to additional investors. In contrast, I recently funded a startup that's trying to solve Type 2 diabetes, a very simple story. In just fifteen or twenty minutes, those founders can describe the problem they're solving, the people who will benefit, how they plan to overcome obstacles, and a compelling vision of future success. That story has a clear beginning, middle, and end, like a good movie.

One trap to avoid is talking about your valuation goals during the pitch. Some negotiating experts suggest putting out a big number early on to "anchor" the discussion, but that won't work with VCs. Focus on telling your story, and we will bring up our proposed valuation when the process gets to that point. Otherwise, it's a little like asking someone to marry you on the first date.

Before a pitch meeting, I sometimes ask my assistant to come in after a half hour and announce that I have an urgent call. If the presenter is floundering at that point, I may excuse myself and let my junior colleagues finish without me. But if the presenter has been clear and compelling, I'll decline that "urgent call" and stay. I'll decide whether to leave or stay based on several questions I've been asking myself while the presenter has been talking:

- How competent does this CEO and their team sound?
- Do they really know this space from their experience at other companies?
- Have they done their research on the market and the competitive landscape?
- Do they know what other companies might be working on that hasn't been publicly announced yet?
- Are they projecting candor and openness, or do they seem willing to say whatever I want to hear, especially about potential obstacles? (We can usually tell when you're pretending to agree with our suggestions.)
- Will they be compelling in future presentations to additional investors?
- Do they seem realistic in their projections of market share, expenses, timelines, and competitive challenges?

That last question often becomes the key problem at the next phase of the process: due diligence.

DUE DILIGENCE WILL EXPOSE EXAGGERATIONS AND MISTAKES

A lot of entrepreneurs hear advice to put their startup in the best possible light, and some even hear that unless they project a market of at least $1 billion, VCs won't be interested. That's not true and can easily backfire. We never just trust someone who promises a $1 billion market—we research it for ourselves. If they put up a slide with some huge valuation, we're going to wonder if this founder is being deceptive or perhaps somewhat deluded. Any experienced VC will know if you are gilding the lily, trying to make your potential revenue look bigger than it really is.

For instance, I was once pitched by a startup that was making a system for biological drugs, which I found intriguing. They said the potential market was $2 to $3 billion. I asked how they got to that estimate. "Well," they replied, "all the biological drugs would be packaged with this injector, and that's a $2 billion market." I didn't need a Google search to spot this faulty logic. If you're just making devices but not the drugs that go with them, you can't include the revenue from the drugs, which are all owned by other companies. Either these founders thought we were too dumb to spot the exaggeration, or they were too clueless to see the flaw in their calculation. Either way, we didn't want to get into business with them.

Most deceptions or exaggerations are less obvious than that example, but they virtually all get exposed during the due diligence that follows a successful pitch meeting. For instance, are there other companies holding similar patents? If so, but you told us that your solution is unique, our patent attorneys will quickly find out. Maybe that means that you didn't do your homework, which is bad. Or maybe you knew and decided to lie or omit the truth, which is worse. Either way, we won't be investing in your startup.

VCs will spend a surprising amount of money on due diligence before committing to any deal. Consultants who know the space don't come cheap, nor do specialized lawyers and market researchers. But it's worth it because our first investment in your startup is likely to lead to much more capital later. The first $100,000 we give you might become $10 million by the time we exit. So it's worth spending, say, $50,000 to potentially save millions—which could be lost if we fail to catch a big problem.

You should assume that VCs will definitely figure out if you're overestimating the market or how much share you or your competitors can grab. We will also figure out if you're underestimating your opportunity, which happens more often than you might expect. Founders sometimes say something like "The total market for this is $500 million, and we will capture 10 percent of it." Then they reveal that they control all of the relevant patents and other defensible advantages. I'll ask why they only estimated 10 percent—why not 50 or 90 or 100 percent? The answer is usually "I'm just being conservative." So it's possible to be too conservative and sell yourself short. Strive for realism rather than either false grandiosity or false humility. I care more about the logic than the numbers.

If our due diligence finds a significant discrepancy from the proposal or pitch deck, I like to go back to the entrepreneur to request an explanation rather than jump to a negative conclusion. "I just found out that there's a Chinese company working on the exact same offering. Did you know about it?" This question is a test of the founders' character. Did they know about that Chinese competitor? If not, why not? If yes, did they think it was unimportant? Or were they trying to pull a fast one? Sometimes our due diligence is wrong. Maybe there's a subtle difference between what that Chinese company is doing and what this startup is doing, so they aren't really competing. I'd rather find out for sure before slamming the door.

Before you assert anything, question your assumptions. For instance, a scientist from the United Kingdom pitched us a drug that would be made by combining three existing drugs. It was a good idea that would fill an unmet need. But his budget and timeline were way off base because he hadn't factored in extensive testing and FDA approval. He knew that all three drugs had already been proven safe and effective, so he didn't think the FDA would need to approve the combination. But from the FDA's perspective, that combo was a new drug for a new purpose, requiring a new round of extensive testing.

Due diligence is often a lengthy process of evaluating the entrepreneur along with the opportunity. Because mutual trust is so paramount in this long-term relationship, prepare to have every detail of your pitch and proposal fact-checked.

EVALUATING A FOUNDER'S INTANGIBLES

Another aspect of due diligence is more intangible—a VC's gut instincts on a startup team's personal character, commitment, and management competence. This part of the process is less about fact-checking than about really getting to know you before we commit. We want to leave no stone unturned about who you really are. In fact, I often joke that I want to hear what your kindergarten teacher thought of you. More seriously, we want to talk to people who've worked closely with you at previous jobs.

You may assume that we'd most urgently want to interview your former bosses, and we do, but I find it more valuable to talk with your former direct reports. There are a lot of ineffective managers who excel at convincing their own bosses that they are highly competent leaders. We call that the art of managing up, or the care and feeding of the boss, and it's a useless skill at a startup. Your former direct reports will usually give a more complete and accurate picture of your leadership skills. We'll also talk to some of your former peers to find out how you treated them.

I remember a few proposals from high-profile, renowned scientists who were very good at their fields of specialty but who made the mistake of thinking they would be equally good at everything. They said, "I've always wanted to be CEO of a company. I know I can run it better than anybody else because I really know the science behind our product." But then a conversation with their former direct reports revealed a history of toxic, reckless, or otherwise disastrous management.

Some founders aren't quite that bad, but our due diligence might reveal that they have a history of acting like bureaucrats, not risk-takers. It's possible to rise very high in a large company by keeping your head down and following the priorities set by your boss and your boss's boss. But that doesn't make you a doer, let alone a strategic thinker. After recruiting some high-profile executives into startups who turned out to be disasters, we are on high alert for bureaucrats.

Another part of our personal screening is trying to gauge your level of passion and commitment. Are you truly hungry for this startup to work? What evidence backs that up? Evidence of deep commitment and passion can sometimes overcome concerns about experience and raw capability. We can teach certain business skills, but we can't teach dedication.

Conversely, if you are holding on to a day job and making this startup your side hustle, that's a huge red flag. I've had some proposals that essentially say, "Here's a great idea, but I plan to hire someone else to run it because I'm too busy." If you want someone else to serve as a more qualified CEO, recruit that person *before* you approach investors so we can fully evaluate them as your cofounder.

At the end of this long evaluation process, I find that the most valuable question I can ask myself is: "Would I take this deal for nothing?" In many cases, the answer is no because of one or more red flags. A bad deal is a huge waste of time at any price, even for free. But if we do want to go into business with you, we will sharpen our pencils and make an offer: X in capital in exchange for Y in equity.

EVALUATING AN OFFER: THE FINANCIALS

Let's say you've cleared all the steep hurdles of a pitch meeting, due diligence, and character evaluation, and you finally get an offer from a VC. Now the ball is in your court to decide if the offer meets your needs and if the VC will be a good fit for your startup. Let's take those two questions separately.

Here's a fact that may surprise you: within limits, the dollar amount of the offer is the *least* important element. People naturally put a big premium on the size of the offer because they can brag about it to friends and family who know nothing about startups. That's just human nature. Founders have also been conditioned by *Shark Tank* and other media that it's all about the number. It makes great TV if a couple of sharks are throwing out six- or seven-figure offers to woo a founder.

But the initial offer is really just a down payment on a long-term partnership. More payments will follow if things go well based on your mutually agreed-upon milestones, which should be spelled out in the VC's offer. By the time you and your investors finally reach an exit point (see chapter seven), the VC will have put in far more than the initial commitment. And that first round of capital will be long since spent and forgotten.

It's rare that two or more established VC firms will evaluate the same startup and reach radically different conclusions about its valuation. Usually, the gap between offers is small, but there are exceptions when one VC might be especially hungry for a deal and much more willing to front-load a big investment. In that case, you need to look beyond the top-line number to study the details of the deal.

Domain was once competing with another VC firm to be the lead investor in a pharma startup. We offered the founding team of scientists $1 million to get them to the proof-of-concept stage, but our competitors offered $15 million right up front, without any intermediate benchmarks. Of course, it was very tempting for those scientists to take the $15 million and have plenty of capital for the indefinite future.

I sat down with them and explained how much better off they would be if they accepted investments stage by stage rather than all at once. If they took Domain's $1 million now in return for 15 percent equity, they'd be able to sell future rounds of equity at much higher valuations, assuming decent progress toward their milestones. Ultimately, they stood to raise much more than $15 million without giving up a majority of the company. But if they took the other firm's $15 million now, they would have to give up a whopping 70 percent of the company to justify the other firm's higher level of risk. I showed them that it's nearly impossible for founders to build serious wealth if they only have 30 percent equity after the first round of financing.

I wrapped up my pitch by saying something like, "If you think this startup is not going to work, you might as well stop now and go do something else. Don't waste your time. But if you think it has a real shot, have the courage to take just $1 million now for the opportunity to raise much more later on, at much more favorable valuations." They decided to go with us, and the startup did very well, eventually going public. It was a win-win for all of us.

If you don't like the valuation that's offered, you generally can't shop one VC's offer to others who might also be interested. In general, VCs hate to bid against each other, and their offers are usually nonnegotiable, take it or leave it. But you do have the right to push back if you think the VC is relying on assumptions and comparable deals that don't reflect your situation. It's appropriate to ask what comparables the VC used to calculate their offer and to challenge them if you have research on your side.

For instance, you might say something like: "I know that company, and they only had two patents and no CEO when they got funded. We already have five patents and an excellent, proven CEO on our team." It's a good way to push back on a disappointing valuation because it's based on facts, not opinions. The key is not simply complaining, "We just think you should pay us more," with no rational basis. It needs to be: "Here are the facts and context that justify a higher valuation." It always comes back to doing your homework in advance.

EVALUATING AN OFFER: THE NONFINANCIAL FACTORS

If you're fortunate enough to have several offers to choose from, you can't simply compare the financial aspects. It's equally important to gauge the nonfinancial contributions of any investor you'll be partnering with, yet most first-time entrepreneurs greatly underestimate this aspect of a deal. The big question isn't who's going to give you the most money but who is going to be the best possible partner for the duration of the startup. Who is most likely to help you achieve your long-term goals?

My friend Joe Lacob, a VC who is also the majority owner of the Golden State Warriors, has a great analogy: "Being a VC is like owning a sports team—nobody understands how important ownership is in the process of building a successful team. People say the best owners get out of the way, but that's wrong. The best owners are *very* involved. Not micromanaging, but helping with hiring, creating the vision, and paying attention to details."

How do you evaluate the help you're going to get from a VC? If they don't bring up those details first, you have to ask questions such as:

- Will you help us find and hire excellent outside vendors such as lawyers, tech experts, and accountants with experience in our industry?
- What's your track record in supporting your startups during hard times?
- Can we pick your brain whenever we face tough questions?
- Can you make introductions to the founders of your other startups for possible joint ventures or other networking opportunities?
- Can you help us pursue licensing deals and other strategic alliances?
- Will we be able to reach you whenever we want to bounce an idea off you, or only during monthly board meetings?

It's possible that a firm making you an offer is purely focused on the financials and doesn't plan to give much support or advice. Some huge VC funds place a ton of bets on a wide range of start-ups, without putting much effort into helping them. Their strategy is that some will pay off big on their own strengths, compensating for the ones that flop without support. That approach might work for the fund, but it's not very comforting for startup founders who are left to figure everything out on their own.

For instance, in the example above where Domain's $1 million offer was up against another firm's $15 million, our competitor was a financial group that focused purely on numbers. One reason the founders chose us was Domain's deep experience and network in our core sectors (biotech, pharma, and medical devices), which can help our startups in countless ways.

YOU HAVE THE MONEY—NOW WHAT?

Feel free to pop a bottle of champagne to celebrate the successful completion of your first round of financing. But your relationship with your VC is really just beginning. You can expect lots of face time during monthly board meetings and, in between those meetings, during informal calls. If you have a good VC, your interactions will feel like collaboration sessions, not performance reviews.

You can expect big-picture strategic help far more than tactical help, unless you ask for more detailed advice. The gist of the relationship will be tracking those milestones you agreed to in your deal agreement. For instance, if your goal was completing a working prototype in six months, the VC will ask how it's going and whether you need help, but the burden is on you to figure out the tactical steps to reach the next milestone. A good VC won't micromanage the money they put in. We generally won't ask why your travel expenses are over budget or why you hired that person for a mid-level job. It's our job to watch and listen and support you from a distance without stepping on your responsibility to manage your own business.

Speaking of managing, our next two chapters will address how to build the team you need to reach your startup's goals and how to execute on the business plan that got you that hard-won financing.

QUESTIONS TO PONDER

About Getting Financing

- Is your startup really ready to seek outside funding, or should you keep working on its fundamentals for now?
- Will you be able to present your startup's compelling strengths without lying, exaggerating, or coming across as naively over-optimistic?
- Are you willing to take the time to research a select group of potential VCs, network with mutual connections, and craft a brief pitch to land an appointment?
- Can you transform the dry facts of your startup into a compelling thirty-minute story that meets the needs of VCs?
- Can you walk the fine line of touting your strengths without sounding arrogant or boring? (If so, you will immediately jump to the top quartile of founders!)

- Are there skeletons in your closet that you would hate to see exposed during due diligence?
- Are you willing to kiss a lot of frogs to find a VC who's a true prince or princess?

THE TEAM
Do Old Adages Still Apply?

SIMPLIFYING PEOPLE AND CULTURE

This chapter focuses on the people who will surround you at your startup, especially cofounders, employees, and board members. You can find a whole library of books about leadership, human resources, workplace culture, and what it takes to achieve goals through collaboration. Rather than try to boil down that library, I'll stick to some key principles that have served me well over the years. Many of them didn't sink in until I learned them the hard way. Some contradict old adages such as "Stay lean and mean" and "Share information on a need-to-know basis."

First: you can't do it alone, so park your ego at the door and accept help. No matter how smart you are, even if you invented the new technology at the heart of your startup, you can't figure out the answers to every question. Any startup is just too complicated, spanning fields as diverse as finance, operations, technology, marketing, sales, supply chains, and so on. Fortunately, you can build a powerful team of allies to make it all work.

Second: anyone who says workplace culture is bullshit couldn't be more wrong—it's everything! As soon as you start building a team, you're also building a culture, and there are many possible ways to do it. The Wistar Institute, a pioneer in biomedical research, built its entire culture around collaboration and avoiding silos. At Survival Technology, our culture was "work hard/play hard." Vanguard, the leader in low-cost investing, infused its culture with frugality. At your own startup, you might aim for Silicon Valley–style ping-pong tables or Wall Street–style formality or something in between. While the "best" choice is subjective, what matters most is that you actually do make a choice rather than let your culture evolve without your proactive influence.

Third: hire for your strategic needs, no more but also no less. This means investing in key people who will drive value. Don't skimp on compensation for talented technology developers, marketing whizzes, or other specialists who can make or break your startup. Then, as the company evolves, so should your hiring practices. For instance, a pharma startup doesn't need experts in clinical trials or marketing until they have a drug ready to be tested and marketed. Conversely, for ancillary positions that don't directly drive value (like accounting or HR), you can be more frugal. There's a time to spend and a time to pinch pennies, and part of your job is knowing the difference.

The exception is that if you run across a truly outstanding person before you really need them, it might be worth grabbing them immediately before anyone else does. Some of my best hires have happened when an excellent candidate became available before we had a clear role for them. Prioritize the talented individual more than the timing.

Now that we have those basics, let's dive deeper into the fascinating realm of leadership and culture.

HIRING FOR CHARACTER

I think the traditional hiring process is frequently wrongheaded, putting too much emphasis on academic credentials, years of service, and narrowly defined skills. You have to look more broadly at people, especially their character. I learned this the hard way after hiring too many people who were perfect on paper but deeply flawed on intangibles.

The problem, of course, is that it's really hard to measure intangibles. If you're interviewing a potential sales director or CFO, you can't simply ask, "Are you a team player? Can you handle the constant pivots of startup life? Can you make decisions amid ambiguity and imperfect information?" I guess technically you *can* ask those questions, but you won't get straight answers. No job hunter will ever admit to selfishness, rigidity, credit-hogging, a love of bureaucracy, or analysis paralysis.

When I was at Survival Technology, I once needed a really good manufacturing-operations person. I hired a guy who had been one of the top ten highest-rated people at the Department of Defense in Washington. But he turned out to be a complete disaster because he was used to working for a highly centralized organization. He was good at analysis but hated making decisions. Whenever I asked him to look into a problem, he'd come back with a list of options. I'd ask which of the alternate paths we should take, but he'd throw it back to me instead of picking one. He also wanted to wait for complete information in situations where we needed to make a reasonable decision with only half the information. After that experience, I was always on the lookout for a bureaucratic mentality concealed behind a glowing résumé of achievement.

My suggestion for avoiding this problem is to copy something we do during the due diligence process for startup funding, as discussed in chapter four. In addition to talking to a candidate's official references, who will usually be former bosses, track down and reach out to their former direct reports. The people your candidate has previously managed will give you a much different picture than will their former bosses, who may have only seen a shiny facade of upward management. Lots of executives are mediocre at getting things done but excellent at the care and feeding of their own bosses.

If you have enough time, talk to former bosses, peers, *and* subordinates. But if you only have time to pick one of those groups, pick a sample of former subordinates. Ask them the really hard questions, off the record:

- Team player or solo star?
- Flexible or bureaucratic?
- Decisive or paralyzed by uncertainty?
- Willing to change when a pivot is required or resistant to change?
- And the big one: Would you want to work with or for this person again?

You're more likely to get straight answers if you ask in a non-judgmental way. For example: *Does she perform better as an individual or as part of a team? Does he follow procedures according to plan, or does he deviate when he feels appropriate? Is she better at analyzing a problem and developing alternatives, or does she land on a decision quickly?* There are no universally right answers, but there are right answers for a particular role at a particular company.

My son-in-law once worked for a startup whose CEO promoted him to CFO after just a few months in an unrelated department. He said, "I don't understand why you're giving me this job. I know very little about finance. I was an English major."

The CEO's reply: "You can learn the details of finance. What matters more is that I know you, and you know what we're trying to do. You're a good fit for our culture." I thought that was an extreme example but a telling one: don't focus too much on skills at the expense of character. It turned out that my son-in-law's relative inexperience was an advantage in this case. During the IPO process, he and his boss broke an investment-banking tradition by insisting on seeing who the buyers were and the spread of pricing, which helped the startup and later became a common practice.

HIRING FOR "BEEN THERE, DONE THAT"

Of course, you will have to pair your evaluation of someone's character with a close look at their experience. It's hugely valuable if a candidate can say they've been there and done that, but experience doesn't necessarily have to equal success in past situations. Someone who was bloodied at a previous, failed company brings a valuable perspective that can balance other people's optimism or naïveté. That's especially true if their well-conceived and well-executed plan was overwhelmed by something beyond their control, like a hurricane or a pandemic.

Of course, prior experience doesn't guarantee future success, even if a CEO has run twenty-five previous companies. But experience at startups is a much bigger advantage than experience at big companies, because circumstances for startups can change so quickly and urgent pivots can be essential. The same applies to all of your department heads—CTO, CMO, CFO, and so on.

I sometimes hear pushback to my advice to hire for experience, on the theory that it can be detrimental in a cutting-edge market. If you're doing something radically different, why hire people who've been trained in the old ways of your industry? What if experience just equals baggage? It's true that you can find some examples of world-changing startups run by people who had never previously run anything bigger than a lemonade stand. But as I've suggested in previous chapters, you are almost certainly not Steve Jobs, Bill Gates, or Richard Branson. The more experience you have, and the more you add to your team, the better your odds of survival.

I once met with three first-time entrepreneurs who had a great idea for repurposing older drugs. They had solid résumés in big pharma but no experience running a startup. As I mentioned in chapter two, Domain refused to fund their company, ESP, unless they persuaded one of their advisers, John Spitznagle, to take on a bigger role as CEO, because he had the experience and relationships for that job. They were able to convince John to come in full-time, and his contributions made all the difference to their eventual success. But if the three founders had insisted on going it alone because their egos wouldn't allow them to defer to an older CEO, I suspect they never would have made it.*

BUILD A BOARD OF DIRECTORS THAT ADDS REAL VALUE, NOT WINDOW DRESSING

Maybe I'm biased after serving on hundreds of startup boards, but I think they are widely undervalued as an asset and resource for startup management teams. Time after time, I've seen entrepreneurs fill their boards with directors I call "window

---

* We will return to this fascinating startup, ESP, in chapter six.

dressing"—prominent CEOs from other fields, distinguished professors, retired politicians, or other celebrities or semi-celebrities. The common thread is that their names and credentials sound impressive, but these directors have little or no experience with the kinds of decisions the startup will need to make. They also don't have a significant ownership stake in the company. As a result, these directors almost never challenge the CEO's decisions or even dig deeply into the details. They're also usually slow to hold a CEO accountable for misguided decisions or inappropriate behavior.

Sometimes a founder who's pitching Domain will share a list of their directors or "board of advisers," and I'll call one of them to get their opinion. I've had cases where they can't tell me anything about the founder because they serve on hundreds of boards and put almost no time into any of them.

To take just one catastrophe associated with window dressing, scandal-ridden Theranos didn't have a single VC or expert in blood testing on its board. Founder and CEO Elizabeth Holmes stocked her board with famous names like Henry Kissinger (the former secretary of state), Jim Mattis (the retired Marine Corps four-star general), George Shultz (another former secretary of state), and Richard Kovacevich (the former CEO of Wells Fargo). All were very smart, but none had the knowledge or experience to question the company's blood-testing technology, let alone challenge Holmes for allegedly using fraudulent test results to increase Theranos's valuation.

Being an engaged board member requires time and effort. Almost all the startup boards I've been on meet at least quarterly, for at least three to four hours at a time. Many of them meet monthly and require various conference calls or committee meetings in between meetings of the full board. They also require significant prep time to get up to speed on whatever challenges the company is facing at the moment. You want directors who are willing to invest that time and effort so they will be prepared to help the CEO strategically and also (when invited by the CEO) fill in any gaps in the management team. For instance, I've helped my startups initiate deals in foreign markets and find additional sources of funding.

When inviting people to join your board, look for experts who can advise you, challenge you, and offer constructive criticism. In particular, look for people with technical or financial expertise that you may personally lack. Incentivize them with equity rather than cash so they will truly care about the company's future.

Once you have a smart and experienced board, you actually have to listen to them, which can be hard for founders who struggle to park their egos. They may point to famous, visionary founders who strongly opposed their own boards and turned out to be right because they were so far ahead of everybody else in a shifting industry. But even Steve Jobs later regretted being so oppositional toward Apple's board during his first tenure as CEO, which eventually got him fired. Phil Schlein, an Apple director from 1979 to 1987, told me that Jobs's undoing was insisting that he had all the answers.

One example of a better path is ReSound, which Domain funded to develop a high-tech hearing aid. The company licensed patents from the old Bell Labs for an adjustable technology that could amplify specific frequencies affected by the user's hearing loss instead of simply amplifying everything. The CEO and founder, Rodney Perkins, was a doctor with minimal business experience. But he was able to assemble an all-star board that included a former CEO of Memorex, a former top GE executive, and the legendary VC Gene Kleiner. These highly experienced operating executives helped Perkins fill in the gaps in his management skills, with great results. Always think of your board as a resource, not a rubber stamp or a source of reflected prestige.

By the way, founders often ask me how many VCs they should have on their boards. It's a tricky question because VCs tend to be smart but strongly opinionated. I recommend what I call the martini rule: one rarely feels like enough, two is probably ideal, and three or more is asking for trouble. It's important that they bring separate skill sets, such as technology or marketing, and not just financial skills.

FIND THE HAPPY MEDIUM BETWEEN HANDS-ON AND HANDS-OFF

The two great dangers in managing a startup might be described as paying too much or too little attention to detail. Micromanaging can drive your people crazy and cause you to lose focus on the big picture. But under-managing can leave you with a shaky or distorted grasp of what's really going on. You have to find the happy medium of just enough involvement in the details to make effective decisions.

Firsthand assessment of any problem, in my experience, trumps reading a secondhand report or listening to a summary that's been filtered (if not spun) through several other people. It's often worth taking extra time to personally investigate the reality on the ground.

For instance, when I was running Rorer, I wanted an unfiltered sense of what our customers thought about our products. Rather than commissioning a survey or focus group, I spent a full day answering phones in our customer-service center. It was quite an eye-opening experience. Our reps had been taught to follow a script that branched off according to an algorithm. If a customer complained about a defective product, the reps were supposed to respond that it was highly unusual and probably not really a defect. In other words, they were taught to call the customer a liar. Meanwhile, they were supposed to check the database to see if this customer had ever complained before. If not, they could offer a free replacement.

After my day in the call center, I asked our customer-service manager to get rid of the rigid algorithms and instead train representatives to use their judgment, case by case. The attitude I wanted to encourage was, "Treat the customer the way you would like to be treated if you had the same problem."

I've found that rigid procedures are usually created by managers who are too focused on maintaining control and covering their asses rather than serving customers and delivering results. It's as if they think they're safe if they enforce an approved way of doing things, even if frontline staff and customers hate the bureaucratic rulebook. They behave as if accountability has no connection to results. So my solution in this case was to get more hands-on in gathering information but simultaneously more hands-off in telling our people how to do their jobs.

DELEGATE DECISIONS TO EXPERTS AND AVOID SECRECY AS MUCH AS POSSIBLE

It's another myth that the boss should make all the hard calls. If you delegate some key decisions to those who are more knowledgeable about the relevant details, you'll wind up with better outcomes while making people feel empowered and valued.

When I was president of Rorer, we acquired the healthcare division of Revlon as part of a complex multiparty deal.* It was the biggest and most expensive merger I've ever been involved in, making me responsible for another $700 million or so in revenue, plus a lot of new staffers. The integration process taught me a lot about management in general, not just about mergers.

After the deal closed, I spent time studying other mergers in other fields where two similar businesses were integrated. Bank mergers were of particular interest because so many of them

---

* We will return to the background of this merger as an execution story in chapter six.

seemed to end badly. It seemed like 80 percent of all mergers and acquisitions never achieved their goals. I asked my team to research examples of both failed and successful integrations, and we summarized what appeared to be the four key steps to botching a merger integration:

1. Make no changes at all while you "let the dust settle." Both companies operate as before while a small group of senior execs plans the restructuring.
2. Winner takes all—the acquiring company gets all the plum management jobs, while the acquired company takes a disproportionate share of layoffs.
3. Plan changes to various departments without their department heads having any voice. Senior management decides everything.
4. Keep all information about the process top secret on a need-to-know basis.

Now that we knew what *not* to do, we planned our integration with Revlon's healthcare unit to do the exact opposite. First, we didn't let the dust settle. From day one, we acknowledged that the merger would require cuts to our total headcount. However, we promised that anyone laid off at the end of the integration process would get six to twelve months' severance, which became a major retention tool. Instead of looking for a new job immediately, everyone had an incentive to stick around, help the merger succeed, and then either get a good new job or six to twelve months of severance.

Second, we promised that it wouldn't be "winner takes all"—all job decisions and policy decisions would be based on merit, even though the CEO and president of the newly combined company would be coming from the Rorer side. We set up nearly one thousand small task forces to evaluate every question, from the extremely important (such as which salespeople would remain) to the trivial (such as what the new expense report should look like). These groups were balanced between Revlon and Rorer people, and I personally checked up on many of them to make sure they weren't playing favorites. The new staff at the end of the integration wound up being an almost equal mix of Revlon and Rorer.

Third, we encouraged each task force to make decisions rather than kick questions upstairs to senior management. After all, the people on the front lines of each department had more detailed information and were closer to the action. This authority also gave the task-force leaders from both Rorer and Revlon a sense of ownership in the outcome since they wouldn't be able to blame management after the integration. We also urged them to move quickly, on the theory that dragging out the process to try to do everything perfectly would only maximize the anxiety of all involved. Within a few months, all personnel decisions were figured out.

Finally, I announced that all communication would be "as soon as I know" rather than "need to know." As each task force completed its work and resolved its issues, from warehouse closings to product changes, I sent around a memo. We mostly managed to stay ahead of the rumor mill that inevitably pops up when layoffs are expected. I was even accused of boring people with all those "as soon as I know" memos!

In the end, we made it into the 20 percent of mergers that didn't flop, and the value of the combined company increased 300 percent in the next few years. We tracked the people we had to lay off and found that nearly all of them got new jobs before their severance expired. In my experience, transparent and inclusive leadership virtually always beats the secretive and autocratic alternative.

MANAGE WITH FLEXIBILITY, NOT RIGID METRICS AND POLICIES

First-time bosses often hear that they need to establish clear metrics for success, such as a system of Key Performance Indicators (KPIs). I've found that staying flexible about goals can be much more effective, however. Rigid goals can quickly become obsolete.

Setting goals for your staff is fine, but structured performance reviews can hurt their motivation to be agile in rapidly changing situations. The best performance conversations are continuous and informal, an ongoing dialogue, a conversation over a cup of coffee, rather than an annual test. It's vital to develop a close connection with all of your direct reports. Stay consistent with your goals yet nimble enough to change course as needed.

According to a survey by Deloitte, 58 percent of executives believe that their current performance-management approach drives neither employee engagement nor high performance.[1]

As an article in the *Harvard Business Review* puts it, "They, and we, are in need of something nimbler, real-time, and more individualized—something squarely focused on fueling performance in the future rather than assessing it in the past."[2]

Avoiding rigid performance metrics relates to what I said above about avoiding rigid policies. I find it fascinating that most employees grumble about strict procedures, but after you take away the policy book, some will grumble even more. Such negativity can poison the dynamic of any team. Some find that rather than being expected to respond to constant change and being held accountable for results, following a predictable, by-the-book process is easier. At Rorer, we threw away our policy and procedure books and established a single new policy: "Use your judgment."

Loosening the reins can also make it obvious who might be too much of a rigid rule follower and who's really cut out for startup life.

COMPENSATE WITH EQUITY TO DRIVE A SENSE OF OWNERSHIP

Big companies love precise job descriptions that keep people in distinct silos. Everyone knows what you're responsible for and—perhaps more importantly—what you're not responsible for. If some other department or division is struggling, big-company employees might feel bad, but they won't feel existential dread about their own steady paycheck. A startup has the opposite culture because anything that can hurt the enterprise can potentially kill everyone's jobs. So in a good startup, everyone feels responsible for the whole enterprise, not just their narrow role or department.

There may be no better way to create that team spirit than by giving generous equity grants to key employees, well beyond the cofounders. Once you're a significant shareholder rather than merely a salaried employee, you look at every aspect of the business with an eye toward improvement. You never say, "It's not my job" or "It's none of my business." A raise can make you feel better about yourself, but equity makes you think like an owner.

Imagine that you're a department head and your department has grown too big relative to its current contribution to the company. If your compensation has little or no connection with valuation, you will probably resist any layoff to protect your people. But as an equity holder, you will probably agree to downsizing and reallocating resources to other parts of the company.

In practice, pre-IPO startups usually use stock-option grants rather than actual shares of equity because the reward is based on improvement over the current status. While you can't track the daily stock price of a private company, you can see the value of your options rise or fall, perhaps dramatically, every time the startup accepts a new funding round at a new valuation. You have a long-term incentive to stick with the company and do everything possible to help it go public so you can eventually unlock your (hopefully) growing wealth.

A startup usually can't afford the big salaries and bonuses that large companies offer to talented recruits. Equity levels the playing field and enables founders to hire and reward great people.

Some VCs suggest limiting equity to a small group of managers who are making key decisions, but I encourage granting stock options as widely as possible. They can contribute to a culture of teamwork from top to bottom.

Don't become an equity hoarder or a "dilution freak" who worries about issuing too many stock options. Problems caused by over-dilution are extremely rare, and an experienced board will never let you get to the danger zone.

If your real fear is watching your equity stake fall below 50 percent, you'll have to let that go. Trying to preserve your job security by being able to outvote the board or the shareholders can lead to all kinds of problems. Some founders start focusing on goals other than maximizing shareholder value to maintain their majority stake. Or they embrace a scheme of dual class shares (voting and non-voting), which can create harmful gaps between ownership and accountability. Giving staff second-tier equity that doesn't include voting rights can breed resentment rather than team spirit.

STAND UP FOR YOUR TEAM IN THE FACE OF ADVERSITY

The lionization of the tough boss implies that your most important role is holding your people accountable for standards and commitments. What's often missed is that it's just as important to stand up for your people in the face of outside threats. A tough regulatory experience at STI taught me that a key part of leadership is motivating employees in the face of adversity. If you have their backs against external threats (assuming they haven't done anything wrong), they will in turn have your back.

STI's big innovation was the auto-injector pen, which made it easy for people with no medical training to deliver injections, without having to measure or fill a syringe. Years before our product became the EpiPen for allergy victims, it drew the interest of the US Department of Defense (DOD) as a tool for soldiers on the battlefield. The Army had captured samples of an antidote to Russian nerve gas, and they asked STI to reverse-engineer the antidote and mass-produce it in auto-injectors. This was a huge opportunity for us, since we had fewer than fifty staffers at the time.

Knowing how tough the FDA could be on drug manufacturers, it was important to me that our contract made the DOD financially responsible for the implications of any FDA oversight actions. The DOD believed we were making a military product to protect troops from chemical warfare, not a drug for the general public, and thus FDA regulations didn't apply. We hoped the FDA saw it the same way.

In a joint venture with a plant in St. Louis that was already making our auto-injectors for an emergency heart-attack medication, we figured out how to produce the anti–nerve gas auto-injectors. For the first few months, our DOD inspections went perfectly. Their inspectors tested a representative sample from each lot, and when it passed, they assumed that the entire lot was in compliance with their specifications.

But then, just as I had feared, FDA inspectors showed up unannounced in St. Louis and demanded a ton of paperwork that our plant had never needed before. Then they did an inspection using a completely different protocol than that of the DOD. The FDA wanted to see the policies and procedures that assured that every batch was made in accordance with their standards. They wanted to monitor every step in our production process rather than simply test samples of the final product.

Soon after that disastrous inspection, I was summoned to Washington to meet with the FDA's head of compliance. Three key executives came with me—our plant manager, quality-control manager, and head of R&D. The top FDA officer and his associates immediately began chastising our manufacturing. They didn't care that we had been following the DOD's standards and had passed every prior inspection. They didn't care that we had never been given any guidance by the FDA. They especially didn't care that this was an urgent military project to protect troops from a chemical attack.

The FDA was blunt: if we wanted to avoid being shut down, we'd have to ramp up to meet their standards immediately. And they wanted STI's president (me) physically in St. Louis for as long as it took to come into compliance. The FDA would send their top manufacturing inspector and top microbiologist, and they wanted me on-site to make decisions and corrections on the spot. This seemed totally unnecessary, but I reluctantly agreed.

Then the compliance head asked to speak to me privately, without my colleagues from St. Louis. I replied that anything he had to say to me, he could say to them. He said that all three of my people were incompetent and should be replaced. I looked him in the eye and firmly told him that we would change our operations to meet FDA standards, but as far as my team was concerned, I was completely satisfied and wasn't going to take orders from him on hiring and firing. The meeting ended on a tense note.

When we got outside, the plant manager whispered, "Brian, I hate to say this, but that was pretty stupid. You're going to need to hire new people to satisfy them." However, I was determined to keep my team, who had the expertise to fix the problems. It wasn't long before I noticed how my loyalty increased their level of commitment.

I canceled the vacation that my wife and I had planned for our fifteenth anniversary and moved to St. Louis for what turned out to be a seven-week overhaul. The staff in St. Louis were encouraged to see me in the trenches with them, even though my contributions were not always helpful. For instance, I wrote the new rules for gowning before entering a sterile room at the plant. But when someone tried to verify my step-by-step checklist, they realized that putting on their special pants would require jumping with both feet off the ground. Embarrassing for me, but a mood lifter for everyone else.

After our next inspection, I returned to Washington for another meeting at FDA headquarters. The second-in-command for compliance told me he was amazed at what we had accomplished in just seven weeks. Then the head of compliance arrived, late. I asked him if we now had permission to resume production.

He refused to answer directly and instead said cryptically, "Brian, the way to express that is to ask me what I'd do if you decide to go back into production. My answer is that we would not take any action against STI." Bureaucrats can be allergic to straight answers to simple questions. I often find them limited to only two answers—"not approved" and "not not approved." They hate to be on the record as approving anything that might go wrong.

I'm glad that I stood up for my three managers and spent those weeks on the overhaul. Supporting your team can generate goodwill, which can pay huge dividends over time. Conversely, if you get a reputation as a leader who throws people under the bus in times of adversity, you will find it much harder to recruit top-flight talent.

A HEALTHY CULTURE COMES FROM REMOVING DEMOTIVATORS

You can find a big stack of books about workplace culture but no commonly accepted definition. It's a complicated and often vexing subject. How do you get an entire team committed to the same mission? How do you generate and maintain excitement about whatever you've set out to do? How do you motivate people?

Some people think motivation is mainly about compensation, titles, promotions, and other signs of success. Others stress employee comforts, from free food to cool office spaces and generous vacation policies. To me, all of that stuff is essentially clutter. It might be necessary, but it's not what really shapes a startup culture.

My theory is that most people start out fully motivated when they join a startup and only lose that enthusiasm when they encounter demotivating forces. So if you want a strong culture, rather than drive yourself crazy looking for ways to motivate your people, focus on removing the annoying or demoralizing things that demotivate them. Some of the typical big demotivators:

- **Mission drift.** You start out with an inspiring and compelling mission, but over time, the day-to-day reality looks nothing like the mission you're supposedly aiming for. Even if your mission isn't as noble as curing cancer, you can focus on the greater good of something like trying to make the best fast-food burger (Five Guys) or creating the best customer experience for shoe shopping (Zappos).
- **Relatively poor compensation.** Money alone can't make people love their jobs, but paying less than your peer group does will soon make employees feel resentful and unappreciated. Even mission-driven people don't want to feel taken advantage of. This is especially true if you stint on stock options while also paying startup-level salaries that are well below those of the Fortune 500.
- **Bureaucratic creep.** Over time, without even realizing it, you can accumulate policies and procedures that don't make sense and choke off the flexibility and autonomy that people love about startups. Systematically look for these hidden frustrations and eliminate them. Most people think policies and procedures are imposed from

above, but often the creep comes from below. Many people want to know that they'll be safe if they follow standard procedures rather than be held accountable for results.

- **Bad managers.** If you see or hear that some of your department heads are being too tough on their people or otherwise treating them badly, don't hesitate to step in. Nothing will drive talent away faster than bad managers.

FIRE WHEN NECESSARY

One of the most difficult challenges for an entrepreneur is deciding when someone's work performance can't be improved by training or coaching and you have to let them go for the good of the startup. This is the opposite of the imperative to hang on to great people. Sometimes you have to accept that underperformers are beyond saving, no matter how awkward or painful that might be for you.

Domain once funded a startup called Trimeris that was working on one of the earliest drugs to treat AIDS. The idea guy was a scientist out of Duke named Dani Bolognesi. Since he had no business background at all, he was happy to defer to us in hiring a CEO while he served as CTO.

First, we hired a lawyer to become a short-term CEO because the startup needed a lot of immediate help to put together its foundational structure, hire a core team, find a location, and so on. Meanwhile, we looked for a longer-term CEO who would be very good at drug development. We found one, and that person ran the company while it developed the drug, got it into clinical trials, and started manufacturing. But it soon became clear that this second CEO was not good at developing alliances with other companies, which we would need to commercialize the drug and drive revenue until Trimeris could be acquired or go public.

So we brought in a third CEO who was better at alliances and business development. Unfortunately, we had so many technical problems that alliances were impossible to execute. Unless we fixed those problems, we couldn't even do a lousy deal to be acquired. We reluctantly had to make another leadership change.

For the fourth CEO of Trimeris, we wound up going full circle to the original founder, Dani Bolognesi. He had been studying management skills along the way, and by now he was ready. Even though we were still biased in favor of professional CEOs, we were willing to give Dani a chance after all the previous turnover. Under his leadership, the company became a pioneer in developing one of the first AIDS treatments and had a successful IPO.

If I had to do it all over again with a number of my companies, I'd be in less of a rush to hire professional senior management. I'd make greater efforts to teach founders without business experience how to run their companies—assuming that they were willing to study, learn, and accept guidance. Assuming, in other words, that they were willing to park their egos.

QUESTIONS TO PONDER

About Leading Your People

- Are you willing to park your ego at the door instead of trying to make every decision and solve every problem?
- Are you willing to put character ahead of experience when hiring? (Hopefully you can find people with both!)
- Will you take the extra time to make great hires a priority and invest in high-quality people for key roles?
- Will you treat your board as a source of potentially valuable guidance rather than mere window dressing?
- Can you strike a balance between being mostly hands-on in gathering information and avoiding micromanagement?
- Can you delegate decisions to the most knowledgeable expert in a given situation?
- Can you default to internal transparency and open communication rather than secrecy as much as possible?
- Will you stand up for your team against external adversity?
- Can you create a workplace culture where victories are celebrated? Where failures are opportunities to learn? Where shots on goal are rewarded? Where demotivators and bad bosses are removed as quickly as possible? Where people are encouraged to use their best judgment instead of following a rule book?

EXECUTION IS THE HARD PART
Least Appreciated but Most Critical

WHAT IS EXECUTION?

This chapter is arguably the crux of the whole book. As I said in chapter one, if you only know about startups from mass media, you probably think the two key elements of success are a smart business plan and a big war chest of funding. The most damaging myth of entrepreneurship is that an idea plus capital will start you on the twenty-yard line. In reality, the idea is the easy part, and getting funded is just the kickoff of a new phase. At that point, you really are on the twenty-yard line—your own, with eighty yards to go. Execution might be defined as the process of getting from your own twenty to the opposing goal line. It's where most of any startup's value is created or lost.

After investing in more than 250 startups over the years, Domain has found that the biggest success factor is rarely the opportunity or the business plan—it's the team's ability to handle execution challenges. Not one of our startups has evolved and grown in a straight line according to its original plans; they've all required a seemingly contradictory blend of focus and flexibility, plus creative solutions to thorny problems. So here's my more detailed definition of execution:

- The *clarity* to distinguish between what's truly essential to your startup, what's optional, what's a relatively minor benefit, and what's just a distraction.
- The *discipline* to focus relentlessly on the essential.
- The *flexibility* to pivot when one or more parts of your original plan aren't working the way you hoped or expected.
- The *creativity* to accomplish your core goals in unexpected, perhaps even unprecedented, ways.
- The *focus* to resist premature diversification.

In this chapter, I'll discuss some of the many possible challenges to your startup's execution, with examples of how entrepreneurs faced such challenges head-on. I hope it will convince you that execution is much more than the follow-up to idea generation and fundraising. If you can hone your ability to find creative solutions to thorny problems, you will truly be on the road to entrepreneurial greatness. And you'll probably find execution to be just as fun and intellectually stimulating as coming up with new ideas for businesses.

MENTAL CLUTTER MAKES EXECUTION HARDER

I believe that the main reason founders struggle with execution is because they aren't taught about it. Most business schools and startup guides focus on the exciting phases of identifying new opportunities and securing financing. You can find a huge stack of books on those topics but relatively few on the details of execution.

Beyond a lack of information and training, first-time entrepreneurs struggle with execution because it's hard to be sure which tasks deserve the bulk of your time and effort. You may want to oversee everything yourself, but your goal should be to delegate or outsource everything that won't directly impact your survival and success. You can start by making two lists: things you do that add genuine value to your startup, and things you do just to keep the lights on.

For example, you should retain a law firm that does lots of entrepreneurial work, including all the regulatory paperwork, and resist any temptation to hire a full-time lawyer or paralegal. You can also outsource payroll, benefits, and other HR functions for your employees. Likewise, don't hire a full-time accountant for at least the first few years. All of these functions, which I call clutter, will become a distraction from your startup's key drivers of value.

Imagine pitching a VC who asks about your accomplishments so far, and you say, "Well, we filed all of our incorporation documents. We launched a benefits package for our employees. We set up a state-of-the-art accounts-payable system." That would be a very short pitch meeting!

The challenge is that we're all victims of our inboxes. The less important stuff may seem urgent in the moment and will eat up your time. You may even feel productive on a day when you empty your inbox and cross off a lot of low-value tasks from your to-do list. But if you don't become proactive about saving your most productive hours for execution challenges, you will drown in clutter. Soon enough, you'll wonder why you're so far from hitting your strategic goals and performance milestones. You have to be vigilant about where your time is going.

THE DANGERS OF PERFECTIONISM

Another big obstacle to good execution is perfectionism. Many founders tie themselves in knots because they want everything done as well as humanly possible. But I've found that the old saying is true: *the perfect is the enemy of the good*. So is a less famous saying that I got from one of my early bosses: *anything worth doing is worth doing poorly*. It's important to demonstrate that an opportunity is realistic early on; once you know that you can make it work at all, you can wait until later to make it work more efficiently.

For instance, during the first year after Domain's deal with Align,* the startup focused on doing additional market research on the appeal of Invisalign to consumers as a tool to impress additional investors. One problem was that we couldn't point to any completed cases yet—Align hadn't been running long enough for any Invisalign patients to complete the two-year treatment. So we set out to prove demand via an affordable but quite imperfect experiment in two midsized markets. In San Diego, Align tried direct marketing to orthodontists via targeted mailings, but zero consumer advertising. In Austin, however, they added radio advertising, urging consumers to call for more information about Invisalign.

The difference was dramatic: Austin saw a flood of interest in Invisalign, while San Diego saw minimal impact. Even though radio was hardly the perfect medium—a description of straighter teeth can't match before-and-after pictures—it was a quick, cheap, and effective way to prove demand. Those radio ads even ran during non-commuting hours, when fewer people were in their cars with the radio on. Sometimes using the wrong medium at the wrong time is the right way to execute.

Likewise, for those support functions (payroll, accounting, legal, etc.), good enough is usually good enough. Delegate or outsource them, and then don't micromanage. Trust the people you put in charge. Keep tabs on their activities at a big-picture

---

* See chapter one.

level, but don't let yourself get sucked into the details. If there's a screwup and your staff stops getting their direct deposits, you will definitely hear about it! If necessary, you can step in at that point. As in college, you have to figure out which classes you really need to get As in and which ones just need Bs or even Cs to hit your overall goals.

You can also contain potential risks with commonsense limits that reduce your exposure. Let's say you're a small startup with $1,000,000 in the bank and a weekly payroll of $20,000. Never let your payroll vendor have access to more than $25,000, to limit the potential damage caused by incompetence or theft. Don't give them unlimited access to your checking account.

Resisting perfectionism will also help you control costs in the critical early months and years of your startup. As a startup begins to grow, management is often tempted to sand off the rough edges and make the workplace feel more professional, more like a big company. That's dangerous because you can easily waste resources on things that won't drive value. For instance, at Survival Technology we refused to hire anyone who insisted on having an executive assistant—an unnecessary expense for nearly all startups. It's also tempting to try to refine your original idea from really good to perfect, even if really good is good enough at this point.

I once had a friend ask me to give his college-age son a summer job in the Survival Technology warehouse. After his son had been working there, my friend approached me (rather cautiously) to ask if I realized that our warehouse was really screwed up. I thanked him for his candor and said, "Yes, I know it's inefficient, but stuff still gets out on time. We can improve it eventually, but we have more important problems to solve first. Unless your son would like a full-time job fixing the warehouse?" (He didn't.)

WHEN A SEEMINGLY RADICAL APPROACH
IS ACTUALLY CONSERVATIVE

Speaking of Align, raising more capital and proving demand were just the start of its challenges after partnering with Domain. The startup's ultimate success would depend mostly on its execution in the face of serious, unexpected obstacles.

For starters, Align was trying to hire a lot of programmers at the peak of the dotcom boom (circa 1999), just when they were exceptionally scarce and hard to recruit. CEO Zia Chishti, whose mother was Pakistani, suggested moving all coding operations to Pakistan. He had connections in the tech community there, and he knew that programmers would be less expensive in Pakistan than in India.

This proposal drew significant resistance from the board because of Pakistan's lack of infrastructure and general political uncertainty. I countered that staying in Silicon Valley would be the truly risky option. I likened it to giving a cancer patient aspirin, a conservative treatment for many ailments but a radically eccentric one if the patient actually needs chemotherapy. Thinking outside the box often seems more radical than it really is.

I suggested we rent space in a five-star hotel with a strong internet connection and excellent logistical support. The ballroom of the Ritz-Carlton in Karachi fit the bill. The rent sounded expensive, but not in the context of how much we would save on salaries; Pakistani programmers who made $15,000 had roughly the same skill and experience as Silicon Valley programmers who made $100,000. With the time-zone difference, our programmers at the hotel could finish each day just as Align's people in California arrived at work to receive their emails. The only downside was that a lot of Pakistani couples lost the chance to get married at the Ritz!

Things were going very well, and Align raised another $100 million so it could move full speed ahead with its US consumer launch in 2000, followed by a successful IPO in January 2001. A few months later, however, 9/11 created a truly unpredictable challenge. Our Pakistani programmers were dangerously close to the home base of al-Qaeda, which the US military would be pursuing. Wall Street wanted that risk eliminated, but moving those hundreds of jobs would be daunting. We also didn't want to abandon our excellent Pakistani programmers. Even though local employment laws didn't require it, I argued for generous severance packages during this layoff, which gave the Pakistanis an incentive to help us manage the transition. We decided to relocate to Costa Rica, which had a well-educated yet inexpensive labor pool, and it turned out to be a surprisingly smooth migration.

Align had started with a big idea, but its first seven or eight years were all about pivoting, executing, and not giving up during tough times. The product kept needing lots of modifications. Orthodontists remained skeptical if not hostile. We had to relocate our programmers from a too-expensive location (Silicon

Valley) and then again from a too-dangerous location (Pakistan). All the potential I saw on day one would have been meaningless without consistently strong execution.

PIVOTING ALL THE WAY TO AN OPPOSITE IDEA

Domain invested in Geron because its scientists had found a mechanism related to aging. At the end of each cell is a telomere, and after each cell division, the telomere shortens. After a finite number of divisions, the cells go into a pre-death mode known as senescence. If the shortening of telomeres could be slowed down, the eventual possibilities might be truly revolutionary.

Unfortunately, Geron's research might have been too big to be commercially viable. Aging isn't even recognized by the FDA or the medical profession as a disease. Getting approval for any type of therapy based on this research would require clinical trials, but how do you prove a lengthening lifespan while controlling for a seemingly limitless number of confounding factors? We decided that even though anti-aging research was intriguing, it had no immediate commercial potential.

Instead, Geron's leadership pivoted to explore the opposite idea of fighting aging—how to *accelerate* aging in cancer cells. Traditional cancer treatments such as surgery, radiation, and chemotherapy attempt to put the brakes on malignant cells. The Geron approach was to accelerate cell division and force the cancer to run out of gas more quickly. Geron made good progress in understanding these fundamental mechanisms, and then we sold the company for a substantial amount, thanks to that dramatic pivot.

PIVOTING AFTER AN INITIAL IDEA HITS A BRICK WALL

I could fill an entire book with examples of startups forced to pivot after their original business plan completely failed, but here are just a few.

The Fortune 500 giant Amgen was originally founded as an animal-health company and didn't find its first blockbuster product until its *eighth* try. My partner Jim Blair had funded the startup in part because he recognized founding CEO George Rathmann as a master of total focus—a leader who could recognize futility and accept that it was time to pivot to a new goal.

Dura, another Domain-funded startup, was founded on a breakthrough idea for combating allergies. While waiting for the completion of a clinical trial that would prove the safety and efficacy of their product, the Dura team decided to license some existing allergy drugs from other companies. Our plan was that Dura could become known to allergists via those other drugs, which would then make it easier to introduce and market our breakthrough new product after it cleared all of its approvals.

Sadly, the company never successfully completed the clinical trial because the weather that year resulted in a much lower than usual incidence of hay fever and similar allergies. As a result, there was no major difference between the treated and control groups of subjects who were prone to allergies. Despite this setback,

Dura's founders realized that they had become adept at licensing products from other companies. So they gave up their dream of conquering seasonal allergies and pivoted sharply to become an excellent licenser and marketer of existing products. The company continued to grow and had a successful IPO, after which it was acquired by a bigger firm. The founders and Domain all moved on with a substantial win.

BAS Medical was launched to license a hormone from Genentech that was intended to ease childbirth for pregnant women. The idea was to relax the ligaments surrounding the muscles used in delivery, making them more flexible. The early-stage product, called Relaxin, wasn't taking off, so Genentech agreed to license it. BAS pivoted to develop Relaxin as an orthodonture drug that could soften the ligaments around teeth, making it easier and faster for braces to move them.

For a variety of reasons, Relaxin didn't find its market in orthodontia, so BAS tried a third application. One of the founders realized that it might be effective in treating heart-failure patients—a high-risk, high-reward pivot. To make it work, we needed to bring in an entirely new management team, including a CEO experienced in cardiology as well as medical and technical experts in heart failure. We renamed the company Corthera and developed the product successfully until the company was sold to Novartis for a significant sum.

Finally, I've mentioned that Survival Technology's biggest product, the EpiPen, evolved from an auto-injector we tried to develop for heart-attack victims. When we hit roadblocks on that original plan, we asked: What other kinds of patients might need an emergency injection from someone with no medical training before paramedics can arrive? The answer was people prone to life-threatening allergic reactions; fast-acting drugs were available, but no one wanted to carry around a syringe and vials for standard injections. The EpiPen became the ideal pivot to leverage our existing technology.

Each of these startups followed their technology, market knowledge, proprietary position, and other advantages, wherever they led. If any had been rigid about sticking to their original plans instead of executing these pivots, they would have failed completely.

USING STRATEGIC ALLIANCES TO BOLSTER EXECUTION

Many startups eventually need to reach out to big companies to pitch a strategic alliance or joint venture to fill operation gaps that require a partner with different capabilities. Examples include a need for distribution networks, manufacturing plants, expertise in government relations, or the ability to sell a product in a foreign market. These alliances can pay off spectacularly if done well, but they also pose huge risks.

For starters, you have to be mindful that a strategic alliance might poison your eventual ability to sell your startup to a larger company if the prior deal might be seen as a liability. For instance, a potential acquirer with top-notch manufacturing will probably be turned off by your ten-year deal to have their biggest competitor produce your widgets. The same might be true of potential IPO investors who will want to see you building your own widget plants if you really want to compete in that sector. Try to avoid getting into any alliance that might ruin a future downstream exit.

For example, consider how drug licensing works in different countries. If you do a distribution deal for a drug in Europe or Asia, it might affect a future acquisition because Big Pharma companies are used to operating globally. Still, given the complexity of launching a drug around the world, potential acquirers will expect any startup to set up alliances with partners who know the local regulations and distribution channels. Acquirers will therefore judge the value of your startup mostly by its US revenue. But if you make the mistake of licensing away your US rights, you'll probably never get an offer. In whatever field you're in, keep the needs of potential future acquirers in mind.

VCs can help you forge alliances because a lot of big companies and foreign companies look to American VCs as a pipeline of opportunities. The big guys can't keep tabs on every startup, but they can ask a leading VC in any sector about potential deals. I enjoy playing matchmaker between big companies and startups who need each other.

There are four potential outcomes when you attempt to negotiate a strategic alliance with a bigger company: no deal, a bad deal, a good deal, and a great deal. It's worth looking at examples of how each can affect your execution.

Accepting No Deal to Prevent a Bad Deal

When I was running Survival Technology in the 1980s, we developed a multipart system to keep heart-attack patients alive until they could get to a hospital, which is the critical period when these patients face the highest risks. It included two automatic syringes, much like the EpiPen that we would later develop, as well as a pocket-sized device that could send a patient's electrocardiogram readings to a doctor via a phone. During a heart attack, a patient could send their EKG over the phone and be told to take one of two drugs that were in the automatic syringes.

We needed a bigger partner to bring our system to market, and I arranged a meeting with Ewing Kauffman, the founder and CEO of Marion Laboratories, based in Kansas City. Famously brash and exuberant, Ewing was then making a name for himself in both pharmaceuticals and baseball as the new owner of the Kansas City Royals. Today, one of his biggest legacies is the Kauffman Foundation, the leading nonprofit supporter of entrepreneurship.

When I walked into his office, I noticed a huge urn of coffee on his credenza, which he kept using to refill his cup. Before I could even begin my pitch, Ewing said in his Missouri twang, "Brian, I only want to do business with friends, and I would consider it a great act of friendship if you bought four season tickets to the Kansas City Royals." Despite the fact that STI was based in Maryland, half a country away, I agreed to cough up a few thousand bucks. It seemed a small price to pay for a potentially huge deal.

My goal was to persuade Marion Labs to pay STI $4 million up front to compensate us for the R&D we had already done on our heart-attack system and to enter into a fifty-fifty profit-sharing joint venture. We negotiated for about ninety minutes while he drank more and more coffee and got more and more animated. Ewing pushed back hard, saying we could either have an up-front licensing fee or a fifty-fifty profit share, but not both.

I pointed out that he had recently done a $6 million licensing deal for a mediocre anti-itch cream, and now I was offering him a much better deal to save the lives of heart-attack victims. Now I was animated too. I said, "Ewing, the truth is I'm offering you a smarter deal than the frankly stupid one you just did." I'll never forget his reply: "Brian, I've spent years flying my ass around the world, trying to get people to see me who didn't want to see me. Even if they did see me, most of them said no. Now, after one stupid deal, people like you are flying to see me. One stupid deal did the trick, but I don't intend to do another one!"

At that point, I could only laugh, shake his hand, and accept that this joint venture was never going to work. We chatted a bit more and parted on good terms. When I got home and went to an STI board meeting, one director scoffed at my report on the trip: "So you failed. You came back empty-handed." I looked him in the eye and replied, "Not at all. We are now the proud owners of Kansas City Royals season tickets!"

My takeaway was that sometimes no deal is the best outcome of a negotiation, and you can get in big trouble by not knowing when to walk away. STI ultimately did a joint venture with a bigger company, Wyeth, that included both our desired $4 million up-front payment and profit sharing.

As a postscript, I later got heavily involved in the Kauffman Fellows Program, an offshoot of the Kauffman Foundation, including a stint as its chairman. I think Ewing would have been even happier about that than about the season tickets.

When a Deal Is So Good That It Turns Out Bad

The same automatic syringe that I'd taken to Marion Labs also had potential for many other injectable drugs. In order to fully commercialize it, STI needed a sophisticated and highly sterile facility to assemble our syringes with other companies' drugs. We needed a new manufacturing partner to build that facility.

I started by pitching KV Pharmaceutical, where I knew the chairman and president. They liked our syringe system and were eager to do a joint venture. I offered fifty-fifty profit sharing but insisted that they put up the investment to build a new plant to produce it. I also asked them to take the hit on any losses while we were ramping up to sell our syringes to drug companies. I was pleasantly surprised when they agreed to these terms—a great deal for us!

KV built the new plant, and we began to solicit customers, but revenue came very slowly. Their unshared losses became so huge that our joint venture threatened to bankrupt KV. STI had to bail them out by taking over operational responsibility for the facility, which was inconveniently located in St. Louis. We also had to take on full financial responsibility after terminating the joint venture. Fortunately, we later got lucky with a large government contract that recouped the facility's losses and started to generate positive cash flow.*

Some say I drove a hard bargain and got a really good deal. Nevertheless, I still see this as a bad deal. Part of good execution is making sure that everyone benefits. My one-sided deal backfired. As a practical matter, it weakened our partner's ability to perform, costing more time and money than a "fair deal" would have cost.

Forging a Good Deal with a Trusted Partner

Prior to my joining Rorer, we had a long-term licensing arrangement with the Japanese pharmaceutical company Yamanouchi. Japan is the world's second-largest pharmaceutical market, and I became convinced that we should be doing our own production and distribution there, not going through a local partner that kept much of the profit. Our lawyers told me that Rorer's licensing deal with Yamanouchi was no longer valid. Legally, we could build our own business there.

But there were two problems with that idea. First, Rorer currently had no capacity to distribute its drugs directly in Japan;

---

* See the FDA story in chapter five.

ripping up our current arrangement without a new plan would be a disaster. Second, I didn't want to poison my relationship with the CEO of Yamanouchi, Morioka. I had gotten to know and respect him during previous meetings because Japanese executives don't cut to the chase in any negotiation; they first take their time to establish a relationship. That was a major cultural difference when doing business in Japan.

I decided to be completely honest with Morioka about our strategic problem and ask for his advice. After that meeting, he came back with a clever win-win solution. For budgetary reasons, there were certain products that Yamanouchi wasn't selling aggressively all over Japan. Morioka offered to license Rorer the rights to sell some of those products in some parts of the country. The cash flow from those products would help us afford to build a Japanese sales force, which we could later use to distribute our own products as well. Yamanouchi benefited by getting licensing revenue for its previously undersold products, and in less than two years, Rorer doubled its revenue in Japan.

My takeaway was that all the extra time Morioka and I had spent getting to know each other really paid off. Our mutual understanding and trust enabled us to find a creative solution that made sense for both sides.

Betting Big on a Truly Great Deal

As EVP of Rorer, I was put in charge of corporate strategic planning as well as our medical-device operations and pharmaceutical

R&D. As I studied the whole company, it became clear that we were too small to adequately compete in the prescription pharmaceutical market. We had three hundred salespeople in an industry where the average company had seven hundred to one thousand.

A possible solution emerged when I heard that two Wall Street players were pursuing a takeover of Revlon, which had three distinct units. A private equity firm, Forstmann Little, wanted to keep and run Revlon's healthcare business while selling off its beauty and pharmaceutical units. Investor Ron Perelman, on the other hand, wanted Revlon's beauty business to merge with one of his companies, Pantry Pride, but had no interest in healthcare or pharmaceuticals.

Revlon's healthcare and pharma businesses were similar to Rorer's in that they were small compared to the big firms in those sectors. They would be a perfect merger fit for Rorer, turning two small players into one strong new competitor. But how could we pull that off, with Perelman and Forstmann Little already in a multibillion-dollar bidding war? My initial instinct was to go to Forstmann Little, since one of their founding partners had been my classmate at both college and business school. But first I decided to seek counsel from our investment banker, Bruce Wasserstein at First Boston, who advised the opposite strategy. Since Forstmann Little already had enough money to complete the acquisition, Rorer could help Perelman win the prize in exchange for the units of Revlon that we wanted.

We went to Perelman's team with this win-win proposal to help them win the bidding war, offering $500 million in cash after calculating that Revlon's healthcare and pharma units were worth up to $900 million to Rorer. During an urgent 2 AM call with the parties, we raised Rorer's contribution to $650 million, which was enough to win. We had no letter of agreement or legal papers with Perelman, just a virtual handshake over the phone. I later learned (not from Perelman's team or anyone at Revlon) that a few weeks after the bidding ended, another company offered Perelman nearly $100 million more than we had for Revlon's healthcare and pharma units. He told them he already had a handshake deal with us, which was not only the ethically correct move but also a smart, pragmatic move. Perelman, who did mergers and acquisitions for a living, knew that his potential future partners would ask Rorer what it was like to work with him.

EXECUTION SOMETIMES REQUIRES HANDS-ON INVOLVEMENT

Armour was one of many small business units that Rorer acquired as part of that Revlon deal. After the merger closed, we learned that Armour's engineers were working on an intriguing new product—a new kind of intravenous bag that was virtually unbreakable, even if dropped from a height of one hundred feet. At that time, hospitals used glass or thin plastic containers for IV liquids, which broke easily if dropped. This new bag had the potential to become a game changer and capture massive sales. Armour had already spent a few million on R&D by the time this project got on my radar.

Here's where geography can hinder execution. Rorer's HQ was in a suburb of Philadelphia, and the lab working on the IV bags was a two-hour drive west, in rural Pennsylvania. It's not surprising that in the first few months after the merger, none of our executives had made the four-hour round-trip drive to visit Armour.

One day, I decided to check on the progress of this revolutionary product, and by using our company helicopter, I got there in a half hour. I asked the folks at Armour for several samples of their new IV bags, filled with water. Then I had the helicopter pilot hover one hundred feet over the parking lot while I dropped the bags out the door, one by one. We watched them splash like water balloons as they hit the pavement.

We saved a lot of money by suspending that expensive project, yet I wondered how much more could have been saved with earlier attention to detail.

THINK OUTSIDE THE BOX

Rorer also owned Maalox heartburn medicine, which by 1987 was a thirty-five-year-old, low-growth, over-the-counter dinosaur. It had annual sales of more than $100 million, but our consultants suggested that we basically ignore it, just collecting profits until its inevitable decline. We still promoted it to doctors, who would recommend Maalox to patients with heartburn, but we were advised not to waste any money on consumer advertising.

Rather than accept this advice, I did some firsthand research. First, I went on sales calls with our reps to see the dynamic when they spoke with doctors. It was clear that every doctor already knew and liked Maalox. To my surprise, most were unaware that we didn't advertise it directly to consumers, and they merely shrugged when I said we might try some consumer advertising.

Our decision to advertise Maalox happened to coincide with the Black Monday stock-market crash, and our ad agency suggested dressing actors in giant Maalox boxes to pass out T-shirts on Wall Street reading, "I'm having a Maalox moment!" This tagline was such a media hit that it became the foundation of a hugely successful ad campaign—TV commercials, billboards, print, the works. Maalox sales soared beyond anyone's projections. The takeaway is that with good execution and a willingness to try something unconventional, any product or brand can surprise you—and the "experts."

HOW SMART EXECUTION CAN INCREASE A STARTUP'S VALUE

I mentioned ESP in chapter five as an example of the value of experienced leadership. This startup is even more interesting as proof that a well-executed average idea can generate more value than a poorly executed great idea can. ESP's business model wasn't merely an average idea; it was literally about recycling other people's subaverage, discarded ideas. I nicknamed this approach "dumpster diving" since it created value from someone else's junk. Domain was one of the first VC firms to embrace this model, which bypassed the very expensive and slow process of drug R&D

and multiple trials to win government approvals. Only one in ten thousand potential drugs survives that entire process, so a much cheaper and faster model was tremendously appealing.

ESP's four founders set out to buy or license existing drugs that Big Pharma companies were no longer interested in promoting. By innovating new uses for these drugs and vigorously marketing them, they believed they could make the drugs far more profitable. All were former executives of Warner-Lambert, which had just gone through major layoffs following a merger. At our first meeting, I learned that ESP stood for "Extraordinary Severance Package"—a private joke about their generous termination benefits, which enabled them to get their startup off the ground. I was immediately drawn to anyone who would hide an inside joke in their company name. Later, we'd use the same acronym for a new tagline, "Excellence in Specialty Pharmaceuticals."

One drug they licensed from Wyeth was a blood-pressure medication that came in both pill and intravenous forms. The pill was just average in performance, and the IV solution was marketed for emergency hospital use. But Wyeth had overlooked the IV solution's potential as a surgery drug; it could control blood pressure with high accuracy and predictability compared to any of its competitors. ESP saw an opportunity to run new studies and rebrand it as a surgery drug. Sure enough, tests proved that the drug was best in class for regulating blood pressure during cardiac surgery. The newly studied drug was priced to reflect its value, and hospitals were happy to pay for the benefits it provided.

By following this model, ESP turned a collection of second-hand assets worth about $10 million into a new business valued at $475 million when acquired by PDL Pharma. The founders stayed with the company long enough to hone their execution skills, then used their proceeds from the sale to launch a new startup. That one also succeeded, as did a third startup after that.

PATIENCE AND PERSEVERANCE IN A FOREIGN CULTURE

One of the most unusual, unexpected, and memorable execution challenges of my career took place in Russia. It started when then Russian president Dmitry Medvedev joined President Obama on a 2009 tour of Silicon Valley and was astounded to learn that about fifty thousand Russian immigrants worked in high-tech jobs there. This statistic apparently prompted Medvedev to rethink Russia's tech industry, with the goal of reversing that massive brain drain. Soon after his trip, Medvedev backed the establishment of a $5 billion VC fund, later increased to $10 billion, called Rusnano. To run it, he chose Anatoly Chubais, a former vice-premier under Yeltsin and architect of the post-Soviet privatization of Russia.

Chubais decided to invite a dozen American VCs to advise them on investing in startups. Someone gave them my name, and I got an invitation to join this group for a junket to Moscow. I had no intention of doing any business in Russia, but I was curious to see a country I'd never visited and flattered that anyone would want my opinion on how to spend $5 billion.

The people I met in Russia were not what I had expected from the old Cold War stereotypes. Chubais spoke openly about issues like respecting intellectual property and fighting against corruption. We met with leaders in education, the arts, and politics, as well as the business community. We even met with President Medvedev at his house, which turned out to be much more substantive than the quick photo op I was anticipating. He was deeply engaged with us for nearly an hour with his interpreter and staff.

I shared my view that Silicon Valley isn't really a place; it's a mindset. Instead of offering modest tax incentives or government grants, which wouldn't have a big impact on startup founders, the government's role should be to set an atmosphere for entrepreneurial activity. For example, American business bankruptcy laws lower personal risk. Almost no one would risk launching a startup if they had to put their house, car, and family savings in jeopardy. Similarly, celebrating success and forgiving failure needed to become part of Russia's post-communist culture.

Despite my initial reluctance, that trip made me think about possible strategic alliances in Russia. I contacted Tatiana Saribekian, one of my students at San Diego State University, who was a Russian immigrant with dual citizenship and had launched a startup in Russia. I discussed the possibilities with her and her son, Sam. What struck me was that the country had largely ceded its pharmaceutical industry to Eastern Europe. At the same time, because of the financial crisis, Domain had many high-potential startups whose funding sources were now in jeopardy. Maybe we could solve each other's problems. Rusnano had plenty of investment capital but few startups to invest in, while Domain had plenty of startups but a shortage of financing options. True synergy: one party with lots of money but no new ideas; the other with lots of ideas but no money! We still argue about who came up with the concept that Rusnano could coinvest in our startups and that, in return, we would help them build a new pharmaceutical company in Russia.

We came up with a plan to ask Rusnano to co-fund the twenty-one companies that we identified. Those companies needed $700 million total. We proposed that they invest $350 million in return for equity in those companies as well as the intellectual property for the products of those startups in Russia and the former Soviet states. A new Russian company would be owned fifty-fifty by Rusnano and a newly formed Domain Russia Investments (DRI) wholly owned by Domain. I was lucky to hire Tatiana to be the CEO of DRI, and she began negotiating every aspect of the deal, refining processes and procedures to integrate an American VC firm with a large bureaucratic government—a herculean task but with significant support from both sides.

It turned out to be a two-year process, requiring multiple trips back to Moscow, because there was no Russian precedent for this kind of deal. I vividly remember one meeting where we faced Rusnano's board of fifteen notable business leaders and ministers of major government departments. Russians tend to be very direct, which can be both refreshing and challenging. The board's answers sounded so harsh (at least via our translator) that when we left that meeting, I was sure the plan was dead. But Chubais thought we still had a 60 percent chance of approval, and he took us out for vodka and dinner to celebrate.

Ultimately, the deal was approved, with two strict requirements. We had to agree and confirm that our intellectual property would be transferred to Russia and that the new startup would manufacture its own drugs in Russia, not import them. Those seemed like reasonable conditions to balance our partners' political needs with our own business needs. We named the new company NovaMedica and resolved to avoid even a hint of corruption, in full compliance with the US government's Foreign Corrupt Practices Act. For instance, to celebrate the signing of the launch documents, I bought Chubais a fancy new pen—and spent more than the value of the pen on lawyers, just to confirm that the gift was legal.

Since so few Russians had any experience in pharmaceuticals, hiring posed another big challenge. We agreed to hire a Russian CEO with general business experience (in healthcare and telecom), backed by a COO who came from a Big Pharma company in France. The rest of the startup team was a similar blend of Russians and Westerners. Chubais became board chairman, and I became vice chairman. Rusnano and Domain maintained a fifty-fifty split of board seats, even after Rusnano later invested more cash into NovaMedica.

The partnership wound up benefiting everyone and became a case study for creative startup financing in a developing market. NovaMedica had its fits and starts but continues to operate, after adding many products and negotiating a significant partnership with Pfizer, which lasted until economic factors surrounding the pricing of hospital products made it untenable. As the 2020s began, however, the Russian political forces that had been a wind at our backs shifted to become an even bigger wind in our faces. We had to negotiate an amicable exit, trading our ownership in NovaMedica for Rusnano's remaining ownership in a number of Domain companies.

My experience in Russia reinforced several of my core beliefs about execution. First was the value of perseverance, which includes not being shy about going to the top when necessary. It would have been easy to give up at any point during the two-year negotiations and approvals process, or to be afraid to challenge powerful people like Chubais and Medvedev. While I still believe that you can forge alliances by starting with lower-level people at potential partners, sometimes there's no substitute for making your case to the top of the food chain.

Second, Russia reinforced the importance of investing extensive time and research when preparing for a partnership or any other kind of strategic alliance. I've found that many American executives and entrepreneurs get overconfident, thinking they can wing it during any negotiation. Doing a deal on the back of a napkin at an initial dinner meeting sounds exciting but rarely works. Failure to fully understand the other party's needs and motivations—especially if they come from a foreign culture with very different customs and values—can doom your partnership before it gets off the ground.

Third, you have to remember that entrepreneurial attitudes usually matter more than technical expertise. Despite a smart population and an education system that focuses on STEM subjects, Russia has struggled to build an entrepreneurial base like Silicon Valley or similar startup hubs like Austin, Seattle, Boston, or San Diego. If you ever try to partner with an organization whose mindset is bureaucratic rather than entrepreneurial, expect some tough roadblocks before you get to the finish line.

QUESTIONS TO PONDER

About Execution

- Which two or three factors will make your startup distinctive and deliver the most value to your customers? How can you focus more on those key factors and reduce the mental clutter that might be distracting you?
- Are you prone to perfectionism? Are you trying to get straight As, or are you comfortable getting Bs and Cs in some areas that don't matter much?
- If you have a technical or strategic problem outside your area of expertise, are you open to solutions from your team, your board, or outside experts?

- Do you have a trusted adviser to help you stiffen your spine when hard decisions, like layoffs, have to be made?
- Are you so closely tied to your original business plan that you might resist pivoting when necessary?
- Are you willing to think far outside the box to solve a thorny problem, such as by moving your programmers to a hotel in Pakistan? If not, who can help you widen your sense of what's possible?

ENDGAMES

The Good (IPO, Acquisition), the Bad (Bankruptcy, Living Dead), and the Ugly (You're Out!)

START THINKING ABOUT THE END AT THE BEGINNING

This chapter explores the end of your startup journey, whether it happens within a few months or after several decades, accompanied by tears or champagne. There's a lot of misinformation about exit strategies, which often leads first-time entrepreneurs to unhelpful or potentially destructive fantasies.

For instance, some dream of staying in charge of their startup for decades, like Bill Gates or Phil Knight, long after it grows into a publicly traded Fortune 500 behemoth. Others dream of making a quick killing—a twelve- to eighteen-month sprint to develop a product or service or business model that's so compelling, some corporate giant will pay billions to absorb it. Still others dream of staying more modest in scale but keeping control of the business forever so they can pass it down to their children. Alas, all of these outcomes are highly unlikely in the real world.

Instead, there are many potentially good ways to end your entrepreneurial journey and set yourself up for the next phase of your life. There are also some less pleasant ways, like having to shut down your startup, but even those don't have to be a disaster. Let's explore all the possible outcomes and separate fact from fantasy. Along the way, I urge you to keep an open mind about your future options. Sometimes the only real obstacle to a satisfying startup outcome is the rigid expectations of a founder.

STAYING PRIVATE IS USUALLY IMPOSSIBLE

When deciding whether to invest in a startup, one red flag I look for is whether the entrepreneur cares more about getting rich or becoming famous, at least within their industry. Sometimes both are possible, but those goals are much more likely to conflict with each other. If I get the sense that you mainly want to brag to friends and colleagues about starting a company and remain CEO indefinitely, the bar will be very high for my willingness to invest.

VCs get their investment capital from limited partners, who trust us with their money for a defined period, usually ten years for each investment fund we raise. We have a fiduciary responsibility to get the best possible return for those investors before the term of the fund expires. That means that if we fund your startup, the clock is ticking for us to cash out profitably, ideally within seven years, via a public stock offering or an acquisition. We need a clean way to sell our equity stake, repay our investors, and move on to new startups in our next fund. Keeping your startup private forever is a nonstarter for VCs because we can't cash out if it stays private. We would also be blocked from cashing out if you insist that any acquisition or IPO has to retain you as CEO forever.

If the part of startup life that you love most is the ego boost of being CEO, we will have a big problem ahead. Some of the best possible exit strategies, especially a pre-IPO acquisition, will almost certainly take away your CEO title. The same is true if your company eventually needs to transition to a more experienced CEO, either before or especially after you go public.

You may protest that you became an entrepreneur to build a sustainable business, run it as an unchallenged boss, and eventually pass it on to your kids when you retire. Those are understandable and achievable goals, but only if you self-finance the startup until you generate enough profit to cover all of your expenses, a path known as bootstrapping. Your growth may be extremely slow or nonexistent, but if you can make that kind of business work, no one has a right to criticize you.

The downside, however, is that you won't be able to accept any investment capital. You can't pitch VCs when short of cash, because the minute you sign a contract to accept VC money, you're committing to either going public or selling to another company. You might think of your startup as your baby, but if you take outside capital, your baby will soon grow up and escape your control. The key question you have to ask yourself is: Would you rather own and control all of something small, or a piece of something that can potentially get very big? There is no right answer. It's a personal preference.

The sooner you accept this tradeoff, the better off you'll be, both financially and emotionally. Year after year, I warn new founders about the consequences of partnering with VCs. Some of them shrug it off, accept our investment, and then regret it a few years later when they finally grasp that staying private is no longer a viable option.

AIMING FOR A MERGER OF EQUALS

Less common than the fantasy of staying private is the fantasy of growing dramatically by doing a merger of equals with one of your rivals. For some founders, telling people, "We merged with Company X" sounds more dignified and prestigious than saying, "We were bought by Company X."

Every so often, you'll hear about a true fifty-fifty merger that is announced with the promise of fantastic synergy. *1 + 1 will be greater than 2!* I've found that these mergers rarely work out, because conflicts of vision and strategy force one side or the other to take charge. In the turmoil that follows, 1 + 1 usually ends up being worth significantly less than 2. This is especially true when a merger of two struggling companies is a desperate response to declining market conditions. If one rock won't float, two rocks tied together definitely won't float.

As with every rule of thumb in this this book, there are exceptions. I once funded and served as chairman of Univax, a company trying to solve hospital infections. We did a merger of equals with another like-sized company in our field, Nabi. I joined the merged board of directors as the merged company grew, thrived, and went public. So a merger of equals can work in theory, but I strongly discourage you from counting on it. The key analysis is quantifying synergy. Too many founders focus on getting a "good deal" when doing a merger, but without significant synergy, you'll just become bigger, not more profitable. Your equity value probably won't increase enough to be worth it.

Frankly, if you need a "good deal" to make the numbers work, don't do it. If the numbers look great with an okay deal, go for it—because that means there will still be enough synergy even if you make mistakes and need longer than forecast, which is almost certain to happen. How often does any kind of project come in faster and cheaper than planned?

THE IPO: OFTEN BUT NOT ALWAYS A HAPPY ENDING

Now we come to the outcome that has the most mythology attached to it: the initial public offering. Anyone who follows business news hears about fast-growing startups that get hyped up for an IPO by a major investment bank. On the first day of public trading, the stock price spikes high, CNBC makes the founders seem heroic, and the *Wall Street Journal* runs a glowing profile. Suddenly, the founders are the toast of the town and wealthy beyond imagining as their equity stake (though diluted by newly issued shares) becomes much more valuable.

When a founder is determined to get to an IPO, that's another big red flag for me. The vast majority of IPOs are nothing like the rare superstar IPO. The stock price might stagnate or drop on the first day of trading. The news coverage might be skeptical. The Wall Street analysts might discourage investors from jumping in. As a founder, you open yourself to a lot of risks that are beyond your control.

Then, in the months and years after the initial excitement of an IPO, running a public company can be surprisingly harsh. You are now completely under a spotlight, hounded by analysts and reporters after every quarterly earnings announcement and whenever news breaks about your company. You have to spend a lot of time defending your past actions and justifying your strategic plans. If you seem uncertain or incompetent during a publicly broadcasted earnings call, your reputation might take years to recover. It's no wonder that some founders get rattled after an IPO due to all the extra attention and stress.

Meanwhile, your post-IPO stock price, through no fault of your own, can go wildly up or down at any moment. I remember having to waste thirty minutes on a call with a Survival Technology investor, on a day when our stock price dipped. I explained that there were no substantive reasons for the drop as far as I could tell. His response was, "The tape doesn't lie," meaning there was nothing I could have said to make him feel better. Investors are never fully happy, and they will vent their frustrations at you if given the opportunity.

Whenever the stock plunges, it will also alarm all the employees you previously compensated with stock options. Even if the company is growing steadily, when the overall market tanks, your stock can fall well below their option strike price. If their options become worthless for the indefinite future, your best people will become more willing to leave before their options vest, and they will be targets for recruitment by your competitors. The company's founders and VCs, meanwhile, will be locked in and unable to sell stock for at least six months. That lockup agreement is usually required by any investment bank so they can market the IPO to institutional investors by promising that the management team and directors won't be going anywhere.

In short, you're giving up fundamental control of your startup, and it's not your baby anymore. You now have many more shareholders who can vote to fire you if they think you're not the appropriate CEO for the job anymore. Your board will have to evolve, adding many more independent directors who might replace your VCs and other insiders. These new directors, often retired senior executives from other industries, won't know you nearly as well and will be less likely to cut you slack when things go wrong. You will also be scrutinized by watchdog organizations that evaluate corporate boards for independence, diversity, and other factors.

We always warn founders about these life-changing, nerve-wracking consequences of an IPO. I like to ask if they're prepared to generate significant news about their products and customer growth at least once per quarter. I'll ask them to pencil in a quarterly report for each of the next eight quarters: What will be going on that will excite analysts, investors, and the media? If you can't think of much future news to report, you might need to set aside your goal of an IPO, at least for now.

One startup funded by Domain looked like it was doing great with a cardiac drug, and it launched a clinical trial that would take a year to complete. That meant no news to report for a full year until the trial's results were ready to announce. Unfortunately, the startup had already done its IPO, which meant that investors and analysts were hungry for news and growth every quarter. With nothing to report for a full year, many investors lost interest and dumped their stock. They figured they could always come back in a year if things were looking more promising.

If it's any consolation, some of the most successful startup CEOs of the past decade have decided to walk away from their companies in the face of post-IPO pressures, despite making a killing and living large. As recently reported in the *New York Times*:

> Some founders of this era took their latitude too far. Adam Neumann's spending and partying got him forced out of WeWork in 2019, even though he held a controlling

stake in the company. And Travis Kalanick's aggressive tactics at Uber resulted in his ouster in 2017, despite his super-voting shares. The rest mostly held on through the companies' initial public offerings. But it turns out that running a publicly traded company, with its attendant fiduciary duties, analyst calls and slog of quarterly earnings, is a far cry from the hustle and thrill of start-up life. Now, as troubles mount amid a market meltdown, they're giving up the power and control they once fought for.[1]

Despite all these warnings against unrealistic expectations, let me stress that an IPO remains a great vehicle for allowing investors to exit while the entrepreneurs still maintain control. In the long run (ten, fifteen, or twenty years), there's usually no better way to grow a startup into a sustainable powerhouse worth billions of dollars. We saw that with quite a few Domain startups that needed a lot of time and stock-market capital to reach their full potential.

THE CASE FOR BEING ACQUIRED INSTEAD OF GOING PUBLIC

Now you can see why I urge founders to keep an open mind about any potential acquisition by a bigger company, even if they have their hearts set on a splashy IPO. There's no way to know in advance which path will ultimately deliver the better outcome.

Sometimes, with drug startups, we explore takeover interest from one of the Big Pharma giants but then conclude that their offer isn't high enough. In that case, we might move forward with steps toward an IPO, lining up an investment bank and drafting a prospectus. If these steps induce the potential acquirer to raise their valuation significantly, that's great. If not, we can continue with the IPO process. Keeping our options open gives us the best chance of a good outcome.

One red flag against investing in Align was that I knew there would be few if any dental companies that would want to acquire a startup that was trying to revolutionize orthodonture. So we had to take a chance that Align would thrive as a standalone company up to and beyond its IPO. Drug startups, in contrast, usually have many potential acquirers and therefore many paths to a good exit.

The decision to accept a buyout is usually easy if the valuation is unambiguously huge, which means that the buyer probably has a strategic hole it urgently needs to fill. In those cases, the obvious right answer is to take the offer, and most founders will agree, even if reluctantly. But it's a harder decision when the price offered is fair but not wildly overvalued, which is the much more common scenario.

In many cases, the founder will try to reject a fair offer by saying it's not enough money. Here's where emotions often outweigh finance and risk analysis. A founder who has spent years of their life nurturing a startup, driven by a vision of a triumphant IPO, may have a hard time accepting a check and walking away. They'll still see the startup as their baby, and how can they put a price tag on their baby?

I have to gently remind this type of founder of our agreement when Domain invested—that we have to strongly consider any exit option that makes sense for our own investors. Many founders understand the implications of that agreement when they sign it, but later the consequences seem too hard to bear. I'll also remind them of the risks of rejecting a bird in the hand to chase two in the bush. If we reject a fair offer and wait another year or two for an IPO, maybe things will go great and the startup will go public at a much higher valuation. But it's also quite possible that we'll have a much lower valuation because there are always unknowns.

On extremely rare occasions, a board has to outvote a stubborn founder who can't be persuaded to accept a fair acquisition offer. I don't think that's ever happened to a Domain startup, and I'd consider it a failure by the VC to clearly explain the realities of the startup game before they made binding commitments to each other.

THE OPTION OF "EXITING WITHOUT EXITING"

Another reason some founders resist an acquisition is that they can't stomach the thought of running their startup as a division of a huge, bureaucratic corporation. Many of them had quit the Fortune 500 specifically to get away from that kind of culture. They have no interest in becoming middle managers again, even after cashing a big acquisition check. They can't shake the entrepreneurial bug. You may recall Cam Garner and Ted Greene from

chapter two, who refused to relocate from San Diego to Indianapolis after Eli Lilly bought their startup, Hybritech.

The good news is that even though a big company may try to
include the services of the startup's management team as a deal
point (at least for a year or two), that's usually negotiable. Domain
got very good at keeping noncompete clauses out of acquisition
deals so we could redirect our best management teams at new
startups. We found that we always had more good ideas than
effective leaders who could execute on them, so we treated those
people like gold.

One of my favorite examples of this kind of "exiting without exiting" is the team behind three great Domain startups—
Peninsula, Calixa, and Cerexa. In each case, we negotiated an
acquisition that didn't include the founders (my future partners
Eckard Weber and Dennis Podlesak), just the startup's intellectual property and operations. This strategy began almost by acci-
dent but later became our role model for many other acquisitions.

Eckard, who truly is a genius at drug development, spent considerable time in Japan looking for brand-new, unlaunched drugs
that he could license and develop in the United States. He started
Peninsula, with help from Dennis, to develop two antibiotics—
one close to final approval and the other still early in the development pipeline. Johnson & Johnson was soon very interested in the
former but not the latter. So we negotiated the sale of Peninsula
and its first antibiotic to J&J and formed a new company, Calixa,
with the second antibiotic as its IP. We also asked to retain the
top executives. J&J resisted at first, but we made the persuasive

counterargument that they would surely want to integrate Peninsula into their own systems and operations right away.

Eckard and Dennis then led Calixa as it continued research and development of a longer-acting antibiotic. Along the way, they found another new product and added it to their portfolio. When Calixa was far enough along that it drew strong interest from Cubist, Domain negotiated the same type of acquisition; Cubist could buy the rights to the main product but not the newer one, nor the services of the founders.

A third company called Cerexa was founded to develop the latest drug acquired by Calixa. Cerexa was subsequently acquired by Forest Labs, and Dennis actually joined Forest to aid in launching the drug. But after completing that mission, he joined Domain as a partner, with the same kind of arrangement as Eckard's.

STEPPING ASIDE FOR NEW LEADERSHIP

It's possible that at some point your startup will be doing fine, yet you'll no longer feel the drive to continue leading it. More commonly, your board may ask you to step down to make way for new leadership that's better qualified to drive the company's ongoing growth and evolution. There's no shame in either scenario.

When Domain studied the relationship between CEO changes and startup success, we found that having two or three CEOs within the first decade correlated with the best odds of success. The typical pattern was a committed founder with specialized skills being succeeded by a professional executive during the growth phase. Either too many changes or no changes in top leadership tends to lead to unsatisfactory endings.

VCs differ in their approach to this issue; I prefer to address it directly before committing to an initial investment. I'll tell the founder that the day will hopefully come when the startup will be fully operational and stable, facing a new set of challenges that will require a different kind of CEO. At that point, I'll explain, the founder should think like a major shareholder and do what's best for the company by yielding personal control. Founders usually agree to this plan immediately, but when the moment of truth eventually comes, many of them have second thoughts about stepping aside.

When it comes to founder tenure, many focus on the rare exceptions (like Phil Knight, Richard Branson, or Michael Dell) rather than the common trend. It's true that Bill Gates continually expanded his CEO skill set, as Microsoft kept growing from a tiny startup in the 1970s to one of the world's most powerful corporations in the 1990s. Whenever a founder mentions Gates to justify staying on, I respond that if I had been on the Microsoft board in the mid-1980s, I would have lobbied to fire him as too inexperienced for the new challenges ahead. I would have been wrong, of course, but I would have been right the other ninety-nine times out of one hundred. Those other ninety-nine entrepreneurs wouldn't have been able to master the advanced management skills needed to run a giant global company.

One of the trickiest leadership transitions I ever navigated was at Align. To this day, I give founding CEO Zia Chishti and

COO Kelsey Wirth all the credit for launching it successfully. They had the vision and commitment to reinvent an entire industry with Invisalign. But as often happens, Align grew into a large operating company with all kinds of complexities, from sales to production to distribution. Before Domain originally invested, I told Zia and Kelsey that the day would probably come when the company would be so big and complex that their experience would no longer qualify them to run it. When we reached that point, I said, the board would have a fiduciary duty to hire a more qualified and experienced top-management team.

First, the two founders began to have problems in their personal relationship, just as I had originally feared. Zia was the big idea guy, and Kelsey was wonderful at solving problems and executing plans. Unfortunately, one of them had to leave when they could no longer get along, and Kelsey decided to pursue other opportunities. But Zia wasn't as effective without her, struggling to execute on the growing company's challenges. Despite a successful IPO at $12, the stock sank to $2, largely because of flawed execution. I convinced an initially reluctant board that we should ask Zia to step down.

Since Zia was still a major shareholder, I appealed to him by describing how new leadership could unlock tremendous value and make his equity soar. But he seemed to care less about his wealth than about his pride in being CEO. He blocked every argument I made, and after an exasperating back-and-forth, I said, "Zia, if you were me, would you hire yourself as CEO?" He thought hard and then answered, "I guess I wouldn't, but then I'd be wrong." We were clearly getting nowhere.

Just before Labor Day 2001, the board voted to remove Zia as CEO but retain him as chairman. I was assigned to give him the news at a banking convention in New York City where he'd be speaking the following week. Then, tragically, came the 9/11 attacks. No convention, no meeting, and no way we could suddenly fire our Pakistani American CEO without looking terrible. As Zia put it, "That saved my ass, didn't it?"

A few months later, Zia finally stepped down, and Align recruited an experienced new CEO, Tom Prescott. His skilled management and smart initiatives turned the ship around and drove phenomenal growth until Tom handed off the baton to Joe Hogan in 2015. As I write this, Align is worth more than $25 billion.

SHUTTING DOWN THE STARTUP TO CUT YOUR LOSSES

Now we've reached some less pleasant ways that founders might end their time at their startups, but even these don't have to be as bad as you might fear.

Another myth of entrepreneurship is that you should never give up in the face of adversity. We love stories of resilient, stubborn founders who finally break through commercially after bashing their heads against many walls and spending their last penny of savings. But in reality, there's no shame in cutting your losses on a startup that's not working so you can move on to another opportunity. Any startup can struggle for an infinite number of reasons, many of them beyond the control of the founders. If you're inclined to punish yourself for a flop and ruminate about the things you tried that didn't work, try instead to think of failure as simply part of your education. Focus on whatever lessons you can apply to your next turn at bat.

Therein lies one of the biggest differences between a startup and a big company. For a corporate executive, the rewards for success are low (a bonus or modest raise) and the price of failure is high (stagnation or termination). But for a startup founder, the reward for a successful new product can be millions of dollars, while a failure is seen as a learning experience rather than a badge of shame. This dynamic trains people at large companies to play to not lose rather than to win.

Pulling the plug on your startup before it goes broke can require discipline, emotional maturity, and, above all, clarity to read the situation accurately. That's why I ask founders to agree to specific benchmarks of progress in advance so we'll have an objective metric of how the startup is doing. That can reduce the potentially emotional conflict between a founder who wants to keep fighting and throwing more money at problems, and VCs or directors who want to accept the loss and move on.

Since many first-time entrepreneurs never want to quit, I try to make the metrics we set up as unambiguous as possible. But even then, when the key decision point comes, I often hear pleas for another six months to solve whatever's wrong, plus some additional capital to cover those six months. Sometimes it's tempting, but you have to think of that additional time and money as a brand-new investment to avoid falling prey to the sunk-cost fallacy.

For instance, Domain once funded an anti-Alzheimer's startup called Axial, with very tight benchmarks to control our risk. We gave the founders just enough to pay for a preliminary study of the drug, with a binary potential outcome—what I call a "yup/nope" study. The founders agreed that if the study didn't meet our metrics, we would pull the plug. And that's exactly what happened. We had the clarity to minimize our investment before it got out of hand.

There's a saying in venture capital that "lemons ripen early." It's usually possible to spot a startup that will be in serious trouble within the first year. Certainly by the third or fourth year, if a startup is still making progress toward reasonable benchmarks, it's likely to survive all the way to an acquisition or IPO.

THE LIVING DEAD, AND THE REALLY DEAD

"The living dead" is my term for startups that wind up in a weird limbo between success and failure. Maybe 5 to 10 percent of the time, a startup that began with a potentially huge idea discovers that it's actually a small idea. It generates enough revenue to avoid bankruptcy indefinitely, but it's not really growing. It just staggers along like a zombie.

If you find yourself running one of these zombies, and none of the strategies you try are boosting growth, you probably have to cut your losses. If possible, you can sell the startup to a competitor that has synergy with its assets and be happy with a small payoff. But even that outcome might not be possible if potential acquirers find you too small and not worth the effort to absorb and integrate. An IPO will be out of the question, since you won't be worth the time and effort of Wall Street underwriters. You might have to do the equivalent of a yard sale—put it out on the lawn with a sign that says "$10 or best offer."

Finally, your startup journey might end by going bankrupt, which is the worst outcome of all because it means that you lost control of your spending. In theory, if you and your board were keeping an eye on key metrics, you probably could have pulled the plug before running out of cash. I've seen bankruptcies where the signs were clear a year earlier, but the founders were too stubborn and emotionally attached to their baby to accept the inevitable demise.

But even in this painful situation, some perspective can be comforting. If you look at it from a VC's point of view, the most you can possibly lose in a bankruptcy is whatever you put in. But much worse than losing your investment would be putting in additional money (and time and effort) in an attempt to save a startup that's on the road to failure. That extra money would never get to be invested in some other, more promising startup— meaning the opportunity cost might be five or ten times the lost investment.

So even if you go bust and feel like the world's worst entrepreneur, at least you didn't squander a potentially greater opportunity by continuing to throw good money after bad for another year or two. Declaring bankruptcy is not the worst thing in the world. Even if you have a strong emotional attachment to your startup, be prepared to let it go and look ahead to the next phase of your career, whatever that might be.

QUESTIONS TO PONDER
About Your Eventual Exit

- Can you keep an open mind about all the possible ways your role at your startup might end?
- Do you have a fantasy of running your startup for the rest of your life, like an octogenarian senator or Supreme Court justice who refuses to retire? How sad would you be to give up that fantasy?
- Conversely, is your secret fantasy having the hottest IPO since Facebook or Tesla, including a ceremonial ringing of the NYSE bell and your face on every national media outlet? How will you feel if your actual exit is a quiet, private sale to some boring conglomerate?
- Would you rather own and control all of something small or a piece of something that can potentially get very big?
- Do you think of your startup as your baby? Are you prepared to give up your baby to make another baby?

- Do you have the humility to accept that your startup might get too big for your management skills? When that happens, can you graciously pass the baton to new leadership?
- If things are ever looking grim, will you have the discipline to pull the plug well before you go bankrupt?

FINAL THOUGHTS
Advice on Seeking Advice, Followed by Some Advice

As you can imagine, after all these years in the startup world, I get asked for advice quite often. I'm always tempted to lean in and whisper the single word of wisdom that Mr. Robinson gave Benjamin Braddock in *The Graduate*: "Plastics." I resist the temptation because that joke would probably fall flat these days. How many people under forty have even seen *The Graduate*?

When I started working on this book, I didn't want to be like Mr. Robinson, dropping advice that sounds profound but is really too superficial to be helpful. If the 1970s were a great decade for plastics, subsequent decades would be equally great for Wall Street, the internet, social media, and so on. But so what? You can try to chase the latest hot trends and get the timing wrong every time.

Instead of chasing trends, another option for an advice giver is to stick to timeless rules of thumb that never seem to go out of style. For instance, I could have written a book full of nuggets such as:

- Major in accounting so you'll always have something to fall back on.
- Go to medical school because illness is recession-proof.
- Go to law school because we'll always need lawyers to settle our disputes.
- If you like marketing, spend two years in sales to improve your resume.
- Get a job at a Fortune 500 company because it's safer than a startup.

I can't count how often I meet people who listened to such advice and made themselves miserable! They eventually figured out that they hated accounting or medicine or law or sales or life in a big corporate bureaucracy. And because they hated one of those things, they could never be truly great at their jobs. That was certainly true for me at various points in my career.

■　■　■

By all means, you should try to leverage the experiences of people who have "been there, done that" in a field you might be interested in. They can save you a lot of time, effort, and heartache. But whenever possible, seek multiple reliable sources rather than wholeheartedly trusting any single "expert." And always process any advice you hear in the context of the person giving it. I find that most people dispense advice based on their own experiences, and very few successful people are willing to admit that they ever made significant missteps. Well-meaning advisers, even those who love you, will try to steer you down a path that worked for them but may not be right for you. Even parents tend to give advice based on what they did—or wish they had done.

I landed a great job right after college and was promoted quickly to become the youngest manager in the entire AT&T system. When I told my father that some vague intuition was telling me to quit and go to business school, he thought I was nuts. I'd be walking away from two years of career advancement and spending a ton for tuition, on top of the opportunity cost of the salary I wouldn't be earning. I was already married with a young child, so why take such a risk? To be fair to my father, I received the same advice from my boss and my boss's boss, who both warned me that I'd just be setting back my career by two years. (Maybe they changed their minds over those two years, since they offered me a promotion immediately after graduation.)

All of which is to say that the "expert" you should trust the most is your own gut because only you can figure out what will really make you happy, as my grandmother taught me back when I was considering business school. For instance, are you torn between going into technology or finance versus a "noble" pursuit such as the nonprofit world? I can't possibly answer that for you, and neither can your significant other or your best friend. But for what it's worth, I think almost any pursuit can be noble if done well and with integrity.

■ ■ ■

The same applies to trusting your own gut as an entrepreneur. I started this book by warning you that this wouldn't be a straightforward "how to" guide with a clear algorithm for success. There are no foolproof answers or success formulas. You might ignore every suggestion I've made in the preceding chapters and wind up richer and more famous than you ever dreamed. Or else you might follow every guideline and watch your startup die a painful death. So much comes down to luck, good or bad. I stand by everything I've written, based on my experiences, but I know that your experiences will be very different, no matter what you choose to do.

I get a particular kick out of people who confidently quote proverbs or idioms as universal truths. I collect them because they so often contradict each other; every "universal" truth has a countervailing truth in the other direction. Some of my favorite pairs that remind me to dial down my certainty:

- Don't put all your eggs in one basket. / Don't have too many irons in the fire.
- Look before you leap. / He who hesitates is lost.
- Absence makes the heart grow fonder. / Out of sight, out of mind.
- It's better to be safe than sorry. / Nothing ventured, nothing gained.

- Don't look a gift horse in the mouth. / Beware of Greeks bearing gifts.
- You're never too old to learn. / You can't teach an old dog new tricks.

Speaking of an old dog learning new tricks, you may recall that I didn't get into venture capital until my late forties. After a couple of months studying potential deals, I concluded that all my previous experience in running pharmaceutical and medical-device companies wasn't enough preparation for my new career. I felt like I couldn't tell good proposals from bad ones, and it was hard to get honest feedback about my opinions. At one point, my wife asked how it was going, and I said I was noticing that every time I critiqued a business plan, a new version came back from the founders that incorporated my suggestions. "So either I'm God's gift to entrepreneurship, or it's just that I have the money and they don't." We both agreed it was probably the latter.

Semi-panicked about these early struggles, I decided to seek out advice from the most experienced and respected VCs who would be willing to let me buy them lunch. I figured it would be a small price to determine the secret sauce of my new profession.

One was Arthur Rock, the legendary VC who first funded Apple. He told me, "The biggest key to this job is finding the right people. It's all about the people. Bet on the jockey, not the horse."

Then I talked to the equally legendary Gene Kleiner, one of the founders of Kleiner Perkins Caufield & Byers. He said, "Don't worry about finding the best idea. Just pick a startup that's off to a good start and work with the founders on execution. When it inevitably gets screwed up, you can fix their execution."

Jim Swartz of Accel, another titan, told me, "Focus on the industry, not the company or the founders. If you get into the right kind of technology at the right time, a rising tide will lift all boats."

And David Leathers, a pioneering British biotech and life-sciences investor, told me, "It's all about the company's ability to make money. Focus on the opportunity, and don't get distracted by the founders or technology."

As I tried to process all of this conflicting advice, it struck me that their very different approaches to venture capital were based on their unique perspectives, talents, and experiences. Before he became a VC, Rock had excelled as a salesman and was a classic people person. Kleiner had been an engineer and then an operating executive—a problem solver. Swartz had been a tech expert who invested considerable time in studying the details of various innovations. And Leathers had been a savvy stock-market analyst, a numbers guy.

It was like the fable of the blind men and the elephant, each describing a different aspect of something too big to get their arms around completely. Yet they were all massively successful! I had to conclude that there's no single right way to invest in startups or to run them. To me, at least, that made the whole game more fun. After all, if you could succeed as a VC or entrepreneur just by following the steps in some cookbook, anyone could do it, and the rewards would plummet.

Going forward, I focused on leveraging my personal strengths (which were closest to Gene Kleiner's) rather than trying to shore up my weaknesses. Since my partners at Domain still haven't tossed me out after all these years, I must be doing something right.

■ ■ ■

If you're still reading, I assume you've decided that the startup world—the real one, not the fantasy one depicted in movies and TV shows—is the right place for you. I hope I've convinced you that the idea is the easy part and that your journey won't be all about fame, glory, and riches. Along the way, you're certain to experience plenty of frustration, self-doubt, and criticism. So let me leave you with one final nugget of advice, about dealing with criticism, from my salty English grandmother. "Don't climb to the top of the belfry if you can't stand the sound of crows in your ears."

I wish you all the best in your entrepreneurial journey, and I hope you'll make your own unique mistakes rather than repeat mine.

APPENDIX: DOVEYISMS

In my years of teaching and advising entrepreneurs, I've come to use a series of short phrases to make my points about certain key ideas. A close friend, Scott Union, labeled them "Doveyisms." As a parting word, here are some of my favorites:

ON OPPORTUNITY:

"The biggest force is the status quo."
Those who will be hurt by a new idea will fight it; those who will benefit will be skeptical. Even Machiavelli recognized this, five hundred years ago.

"How bad can it be and still be good?"
This is the now-popular concept of the "minimum viable product"—I wish I had branded that idea many years ago!

"Be an opportunity chaser who hates risk, not a risk-taker."
Great entrepreneurs are not thrill seekers at heart. In fact, they never do a deal with a fifty-fifty chance of success; they wait for a deal where the odds are much more in their favor.

ON STARTING A COMPANY:

"Play to win, not to not lose."

Ever notice in sports that whenever a team tries to hold on to an early lead, they wind up losing? That's because energy shifts from focusing on winning to worrying about losing.

"You need to get an A in only a few things— for the rest, a C is good enough."

"We demand excellence in everything" sounds good, but it's completely unrealistic. Why do you need to hire a great CFO when your technology is still unproven?

"Shots on goal take talent and hard work, but goals have lots of luck in them."

I evaluate performance not always on results but also on how people attack issues. Results can take too much time to be visible, and good and bad luck play too great a role.

"Other than success, the second-best outcome is a fast, cheap failure."

Instead of obsessing over improving what you've got, think of a test that will prove your idea wrong. An improved bad idea is still a bad idea! Kicking the can down the road, only to end in futility, is expensive and stupid. It's better to take the loss quickly and move on.

ON VENTURE CAPITAL:

> **"Regret the deals you didn't do, not the deals you did that failed."**
> If you make a bad investment, the most you can lose is 100 percent of it. But if you fail to invest in a great idea, you may have blown a chance at 10X or 100X in upside. Ouch!

> **"Don't fill presentations with best-case vs. conservative-case scenarios."**
> I've never seen a new company hit even their worst-case scenario—because they weren't that good! Really new ideas always require more time and strategy adjustments than you expect.

> **"It's usually the jockey, not the horse, that drives success."**
> There are plenty of opportunities out there but very few entrepreneurs who know how to turn them into viable businesses.

ON TEAM BUILDING AND MANAGEMENT:

> **"Separate project failure from people failure."**
> Most startups that fail are not a reflection of the founders— they are failures of the product or technology.

"The cruelest part of a bullfight isn't killing the bull; it's the picador."
If an employee is not performing up to expectations, either create a realistic development plan or fire them, but don't torment them endlessly like a picador.

"Cars need both gas and brakes to maximize performance."
Any company needs both a visionary CEO who creates some chaos and a prudent CFO who moderates the chaos.

"Beware of 'suits'; they manage up well but rarely work out as entrepreneurs."
Well-dressed, articulate, big-company executives who get high marks from their bosses but low marks from peers and subordinates are heavy bets to fail. Spend your due-diligence time in hiring with a candidate's associates and subordinates, not the boss!

ON OPERATIONS:

"Running a company boils down to three things: (a) do new stuff; (b) stop doing bad stuff; (c) do good things better."
I've never met a management team that can do all three well.

"All activities boil down to either substance or clutter. Your goal is to make your days 80/20, not 20/80."
For instance, emptying your inbox feels good but is really just clutter work. Developing a strategy is frustrating but substantive.

"Forecasts are for taking action, not proving your ability to guess."
The goal isn't to be a perfect predictor; it's to point your team in the right direction.

"You can't save your way to success."
I've never understood the point of "lengthening the runway" or "bridging to nowhere" with more money. I tell entrepreneurs that wasting my money is one thing, but wasting their own time on a failed startup is worse.

"A great idea poorly executed will almost always fail; an okay idea that's well executed will usually succeed."
In other words . . . the idea is the easy part!

ON MERGERS:

"If one plus one only makes 2.5, don't do the merger."
You should only do a merger if the potential upside leaves you lots of margin for error.

> **"If one rock doesn't float, why do you think two rocks tied together will float?"**
> It's tempting to merge two weak or struggling companies, but that never works.

ON CAREERS:

> **"Don't eat your spinach unless you love spinach."**
> People may tell you to do sales for a few years to build your résumé, but if you hate sales, you're likely to be lousy at it anyway.

> **"Make new mistakes, not the same mistakes as other people."**
> You can avoid lots of mistakes by listening to others in your field. Assuming that your situation is unique is almost always wrong.

> **"On the other hand, don't learn _too_ much from your mistakes."**
> I lost a lot of money once by trusting someone's handshake. I was told by many people that the lesson was, "Always get it in writing." But if I'd always insisted on getting everything in writing, I would have missed out on a ton of opportunities. Big things I get in writing, but in other cases, a handshake almost always works.

"Strengthen your strengths; make your weaknesses acceptable."

Who would you rather hire? An outstanding manager who's a mediocre engineer, or an average manager who's also an average engineer? Focus on areas where you can truly excel.

"Pay attention to the experience of whoever is giving you advice."

Do you think the guy who told you to focus on sales came up through engineering? So take every piece of advice with a grain of salt . . . including mine!

ACKNOWLEDGMENTS

I would like to thank all those who supported me in writing this book. It's my maiden voyage as an author, so I needed lots of help.

My literary agent, Margret McBride, encouraged me to write the book after listening to my descriptions of startup myths as well as my war stories. She has been the catalyst for every step that followed, including introducing me to my collaborator, Will Weisser, and my publisher, Matt Holt, while preventing me from making countless rookie mistakes. Margret's colleague Faye Atchison has also provided excellent advice and has gone to bat for me in many ways.

Major thanks to my collaborator, Will Weisser, who not only helped put my ideas into writing but also captured the style in which I expressed them. He's been relentless in striving for perfection, draft after draft, until I finally got bored while rereading my own ideas and stories! Thanks also to Cate Mikkelsen, our researcher and fact-checker.

At BenBella Books, editor-in-chief Matt Holt and his team have been a pleasure to work with, from the proposal stage to publication, far exceeding my expectations as a novice writer. Big thanks to Matt, senior editor Katie Dickman, cover designer Brigid Pearson, marketers Mallory Hyde and Kerri Stebbins, production director Jessika Rieck, copyeditor Lydia Choi, and the rest of the team.

My partners at Domain Associates have been incredibly supportive over the years, always celebrating my victories but never criticizing my many failures. Special thanks to Jim Blair (who mentored me as the "new kid" at age forty-nine!), Brian Halak, Kim Kamdar, Jesse Treu, and Nicole Vitullo; thanks also to my former partners Olav Bergheim, Arthur Klausner, Jennifer Lobo, Bob More, Dennis Podlesak, Kathleen Schoemaker, and Eckard Weber. Thank you, in particular, to my long-suffering assistant at Domain, Eileen Galton, who has been unraveling my logistical errors and organizing my life for so many years!

A hat tip to my venture-capital friends, mentors, and supporters, especially those who were pioneers in biotech: Brook Byers, Sam Colella, Bob Curry, Tony Evnin, Carlos Ferrer, Grant Heidrich, Joe Lacob, David Leathers, Drew Senyei, and John Wilkerson. All of them kindly advised me while I was working on the book, and Brook went above and beyond by writing the foreword. Thanks also to Chris Gabrieli, who introduced me to venture capital; Chuck Newhall of New Enterprise Associates; Gene Kleiner of Kleiner Perkins Caufield & Byers, who took me under his wing early on; and the always helpful Jim Swartz of Accel.

Domain would not exist without the investors and limited partners who have had confidence and faith in what we could do.

My thanks to Rob Cousin, Brad Kelly, Mitch Laubaugh and the Marshfield team, Alan Mattamana, Ashton Newhall, Amanda Outerbridge, and Barbara Piette—all of whom have trusted us over multiple funds. Thanks also to Lord Rothschild and Lord Armstrong of Biotechnology Investments Ltd., who gave us our start.

I'm grateful to all the entrepreneurs we've funded over the years, too many to list here but certainly including Dani Bolognesi, Boyd Clarke, Charlie Cohen, Leonid Melamed, John Parrish, Rodney Perkins, Tatiana Saribekian, Tom Stagnaro, Bob Stockman, and all those mentioned in the book.

Here are some more wonderful people who have provided help, guidance, and friendship over the years—in some cases, over *many* years: Alex DeNoble, who first invited me to try teaching entrepreneurship. Michael Cunningham and Gangaram Singh, whom I met at San Diego State University. Cabot Caskie, Dori Geier, and Napoleon Monroe, whom I met at Survival Technology. Joe Smith and Richard Storm, whom I met at Rorer. Bobby Franklin, CEO of the National Venture Capital Association. The team at the Kauffman Fellows Program, including Phil Wickham, Jeff Harbach, founding CEO Trish Costello, and Jason Green from the first Kauffman class.

Thanks to my brothers and sisters—Jim Dovey, Michael Dovey, Barb Wiley, and Joyce Walden—who were not only so supportive of this book but also of all my efforts since childhood. Jim was especially helpful as a fellow entrepreneur turned VC in the wireless industry.

My daughters, sons-in-law, and grandkids are incredibly important to me, and they not only supported me but also contributed ideas and creative feedback to this book. I can't say enough nice things about Laurel Stack, her husband, Ted, and their children, Scott, Kelli, and Jennifer; Kim Culligan, her husband, Pat, and their children, Brian, Clare, and Molly; and Christy Galloway, her husband, John, and their children, Jack and Elizabeth. Many of them are also entrepreneurs in both business and the nonprofit world. Love and thanks to all of them.

Last but certainly not least, a loving tribute to my loving wife, Betty, who has always encouraged and supported me, in good times and bad.

My apologies to anyone I've accidentally left out. I am truly grateful to all those I've had the pleasure to connect with over the years. I'm very lucky to have a career that's not merely a job but also a fun and rewarding adventure.

NOTES

CHAPTER 1: THE ENTREPRENEURIAL MYSTIQUE

1. Tom Eisenmann, "Entrepreneurship: A Working Definition," *Harvard Business Review*, January 10, 2013, https://hbr.org/2013/01/what-is-entrepreneurship.

CHAPTER 2: GOING FOR IT

1. "Education of the Forbes 400: Billionaires with a Masters of Science," *Forbes*, January 11, 2012, https://www.forbes.com/pictures/mfg45gdkf/billionaires-with-a-masters-of-science-29/#158c2daa6bac.
2. "Education of the Forbes 400: Billionaires with Law Degrees," https://www.forbes.com/pictures/mfg45gdkf/billionaires-with-law-degrees35/?sh=7e2182174cab.
3. "Education of the Forbes 400: High School Degree Only," https://www.forbes.com/pictures/mfg45gdkf/high-school-degree-only-63/?sh=5691f211751e.

4. Mary Ann Azevedo, "Untapped Opportunity: Minority Founders Still Being Overlooked," Crunchbase News, February 27, 2019, https://news.crunchbase.com/news/untapped-opportunity-minority-founders-still-being-overlooked/.

5. Keenan Beasley, "For Black Entrepreneurs, the Racial Wealth Gap Makes Finding Funding Nearly Impossible," *Fast Company*, July 23, 2020, https://www.fastcompany.com/90531094/for-black-entrepreneurs-the-racial-wealth-gap-makes-finding-funding-nearly-impossible.

6. "One Million Black Women," Goldman Sachs website, accessed January 17, 2023, https://www.goldmansachs.com/our-commitments/sustainability/one-million-black-women/index.html.

7. "13 Organizations That Support Black Entrepreneurs," Startup Champions Network, August 17, 2019, http://www.startupchampions.co/blog/2019/8/17/12-organizations-that-support-black-entrepreneurs.

8. Ruth Umoh, "Black Women Were Among the Fastest-Growing Entrepeneurs—Then Covid Arrived," *Forbes*, October 26, 2020, https://www.forbes.com/sites/ruthumoh/2020/10/26/black-women-were-among-the-fastest-growing-entrepreneurs-then-covid-arrived/?sh=7d5af6ac6e01.

9. Maddie Shepherd, "Women-Owned Businesses: Statistics and Overview (2020)," Fundera, December 16, 2020, https://www.fundera.com/resources/women-owned-business-statistics.

10. Sean Wise, Sepideh Yeganegi, and André O. Laplume, "Startup Team Ethnic Diversity and Investment Capital Raised," *Journal*

of Business Venturing Insights 17 (June 2022), doi:10.1016/j.jbvi
.2022.e00314.

11. Ashley Bittner and Brigette Lau, "Women-Led Startups
Received Just 2.3% of VC Funding in 2020," *Harvard Business
Review*, February 25, 2021, https://hbr.org/2021/02/women
-led-startups-received-just-2-3-of-vc-funding-in-2020.

12. Shepherd, "Women-Owned Businesses."

13. "Women in Technology Leadership 2019," Silicon Valley
Bank, PDF file, accessed January 19, 2023, https://www.svb
.com/globalassets/library/uploadedfiles/content/trends_and
_insights/reports/women_in_technology_leadership/svb-suo
-women-in-tech-report-2019.pdf.

14. Robert Fairlie, Sameeksha Desai, and A. J. Herrmann, "2018
National Report on Early-Stage Entrepreneurship," Kauffman
Indicators of Entrepreneurship, PDF file, accessed January
19, 2023, https://indicators.kauffman.org/wp-content/uploads
/sites/2/2019/09/National_Report_Sept_2019.pdf.

15. "Education and Tech Entrepreneurship," Ewing Marion Kauffman Foundation, April 17, 2009, https://www.kauffman.org
/entrepreneurship/reports/education-and-tech-entrepreneurship/.

16. Pierre Azoulay et al., "Average Age of a Successful Startup
Founder." *Harvard Business Review*, July 11, 2018, https://hbr
.org/2018/07/research-the-average-age-of-a-successful-startup
-founder-is-45.

17. Adeo Ressi, "Is There a Peak Age for Entrepreneurship?" *Tech-
Crunch*, May 28, 2011, https://techcrunch.com/2011/05/28
/peak-age-entrepreneurship.

18. Chloe Aiello, "These Eight Start-up Founders Prove You Don't Have to Be Young to Win in Tech" CNBC.com, July 4, 2018, https://www.cnbc.com/2018/06/28/tech-founders-45.html.

19. Martin Zwilling, "Entrepreneurs Who Master Storytelling Win More," *Forbes*, January 25, 2013, https://www.forbes.com/sites/martinzwilling/2013/01/25/entrepreneurs-who-master-storytelling-win-more/.

20. Larry Robertson, "Three Myths About Successful Founders That Just Won't Die," *Fast Company*, October 26, 2017, https://www.fastcompany.com/40483237/three-myths-about-successful-founders-that-just-wont-die.

21. Caroline Castrillon, "How Introverts Can Thrive as Entrepreneurs," *Forbes*, January 23, 2019, https://www.forbes.com/sites/carolinecastrillon/2019/01/23/how-introverts-can-thrive-as-entrepreneurs/.

22. Ibid.

23. Emma Featherstone, "How Extroverts Are Taking the Top Jobs—and What Introverts Can Do About It," *Guardian*, February 23, 2018, https://www.theguardian.com/business-to-business/2018/feb/23/how-extroverts-are-taking-the-top-jobs-and-what-introverts-can-do-about-it.

24. Robertson, "Three Myths About Successful Founders."

25. Deborah Mills-Scofield, "Are Entrepreneurs Really More Comfortable with Risk?" *Harvard Business Review*, September 28, 2012, https://hbr.org/2012/09/are-entrepreneurs-really-more.

CHAPTER 5: THE TEAM

1. Lisa Barry, "Performance Management Is Broken," Deloitte, March 5, 2014, https://www2.deloitte.com/us/en/insights/focus/human-capital-trends/2014/hc-trends-2014-performance-management.html.
2. Marcus Buckingham and Ashley Goodall, "Reinventing Performance Management," *Harvard Business Review*, April 2015, https://hbr.org/2015/04/reinventing-performance-management.

CHAPTER 7: ENDGAMES

1. Erin Griffith, "The Boy Bosses of Silicon Valley Are on Their Way Out," *New York Times*, August 14, 2022, https://www.nytimes.com/2022/08/10/business/silicon-valley-boy-boss.html.

INDEX

Page numbers followed by *n* refer to notes.

ABOUT THE AUTHOR

Brian Dovey has been a partner at the venture capital firm Domain Associates, which has invested more than $2.8 billion in startups since 1988. He has been involved in the development of more than 250 pharmaceutical and life-sciences startups and has served on the boards of more than thirty-five companies (and as chairman of six) with a combined value of more than $25 billion.

Before becoming a venture capitalist, he was an early executive and then president of a medical-technology startup, Survival Technology Inc., which developed the groundbreaking EpiPen to treat severe allergic reactions. Survival's rapid growth during his tenure placed it in the top ten of the prestigious Inc. 100 list. Dovey was recruited to become president of a division of Rorer Group, then promoted to executive vice president of the entire company and later its president, where he led Rorer's expansion into a fully integrated Fortune 500 pharmaceutical company, doubling sales with a fourfold increase in profits.

While still working full-time at Domain, Dovey donates his time to many nonprofit organizations, including as a director and later chairman of Wistar, the oldest medical research institute in the United States. He is a former chairman of the Center for Venture Education (also known as the Kauffman Fellows Program), which has been called "the venture-capital equivalent of Rhodes Scholars," and a former chairman of the National Venture Capital Association, where he launched a new program to promote venture philanthropy.

Dovey teaches business classes part-time, including a long-running, acclaimed course at San Diego State University called "Managing the Growing Firm." He has spoken at many events organized by the National Venture Capital Association, the Kauffman Foundation, the Young Presidents' Organization, and other groups.

A native of New Jersey, Dovey received his BA in mathematics from Colgate University and his MBA from Harvard Business School. He divides his time between the two locations of Domain Associates, in Princeton (NJ) and La Jolla (CA). He and his wife, Elizabeth, have three children and eight grandchildren.